A Commentary on
COLOSSIANS

UNLOCKING THE NEW TESTAMENT

A Commentary on
COLOSSIANS

David Pawson

Anchor Recordings

Copyright © 2020 David Pawson

The right of David Pawson to be identified as author of this Work has been asserted by him in accordance with the Copyright, Designs and Patents Act 1988.

First published in Great Britain in 2020 by
Anchor Recordings Ltd
DPTT, Synegis House, 21 Crockhamwell Road,
Woodley, Reading RG5 3LE

No part of this publication may be reproduced or transmitted in any form or by any means, electronic or mechanical, including photocopy, recording or any information storage and retrieval system, without prior permission in writing from the publisher.

**For more of David Pawson's teaching,
including DVDs and CDs, go to
www.davidpawson.com**

**FOR FREE DOWNLOADS
www.davidpawson.org**

**For further information, email
info@davidpawsonministry.org**

ISBN 978-1-913472-17-7

Printed by Ingram Spark

Contents

Introduction	7
1:1–29	29
2:1–5	39
2:6–23	57
3:1–17	77
3:18–4:18	89

This book is based on a series of talks. Originating as it does from the spoken word, its style will be found by many readers to be somewhat different from my usual written style. It is hoped that this will not detract from the substance of the biblical teaching found here.

As always, I ask the reader to compare everything I say or write with what is written in the Bible and, if at any point a conflict is found, always to rely upon the clear teaching of scripture.

David Pawson

Introduction

God's Word has come to us in many forms and in many ways. It has come to us in diaries, in legal records, in poems and in love songs. But a large part of the New Testament has come to us in the form of letters that were never intended for publication. When Paul wrote to the Colossians he had no idea that he was writing for posterity. I am glad that he didn't, or he might have taken much more trouble with it and he might have made it into a very literary thing. In fact he has not done this – his grammar is all over the place. Verses three to eight of chapter one are one long sentence, which does not even have a main verb. He just got on with writing down the message. The Word of God comes home to us in a much more live way when it is in the form of a letter, for a letter is intensely personal. It comes from the heart and not just the head. It jumps around from subject to subject, but it is real; it is dynamic, it throbs, it pulsates.

When J. B. Philips was translating the New Testament into modern English, he said he felt that he was like an electrician re-wiring an old house, yet unable to switch the mains off while he did so. Now that is a very vivid picture of the life that pulses through the writings of the Bible. If you have ever tried to do any of your own translation you will know that it comes alive and speaks to you. You are handling something dynamic. So Paul wrote these letters, little dreaming that we would be studying them two thousand years later and I am glad they come to us not in the form of prepared papers or published sermons but as real situations.

This also has a big disadvantage, which is that a letter is a one-sided thing. It is like sitting in a room where someone is having a telephone conversation. You cannot help but wonder what the other person is saying in the gaps. Sometimes you can tell, and afterwards my wife might say to me, "So and So's not too well, are they?" And I realise she has listened to my side of the conversation and has put two and two together and made five! She has attempted to fill in the blanks by reading between the lines.

In exactly the same way, when you are reading a letter you have to read between the lines or you will not get its message. You need to ask what was happening at the other end. You have to ask about the people it was written to and what problem is indicated by this or that statement. It is vital that you get the other side of the conversation.

We will begin by looking at a very formal part of the letter. Therefore it is not quite as exciting as some parts of it, yet we are going to get truth out of it, for God has given us this formal passage. There is a right way to write a letter and a wrong way. There are secretaries in modern times who are trained in how to lay out a letter, what to put at the top of it, what to put at the end of it, and how to work out the middle of it. Well, there was a pattern in ancient letter writing too, which Paul observes meticulously.

During the last two centuries, hundreds of letters have been dug up, mainly from the sands of Egypt, ordinary day-to-day letters that people wrote to each other, written on papyrus, which as long as it doesn't get any moisture on it can last for hundreds of years. In the dry sands of Egypt many letters survived all those centuries waiting to be dug up. We know from these letters how they were written. They did not use envelopes, for example. They used a very long strip of papyrus made from the reeds that grew in the marshes and swamps of Egypt. The long strip was written on and then rolled up from the end. Very sensibly, they used to put certain things at the beginning, which meant that, to see where the letter was going, the person delivering it just needed to unroll an inch or two. The roll was sealed and just the first little bit was left open so that it could be read. There the address was written, and there was put the name of the sender – which is always a far more sensible place for it than at the very end. Our habit of putting it at the end is such a waste of time. I open a long letter and may have to wade through pages to find out who it is from. Along with the sender's name and the address of the recipient, they would put a greeting. They described the authority of the sender if he was going to say something pretty strong. They gave the titles to the recipient out of politeness. After the greeting it was the done thing in a letter to say something nice about the people you were writing to, especially if you were going to say something not so nice a little later.

These traditional courtesies and practices are found in New Testament letters. There is usually a paragraph saying some nice things about those being addressed, and then would come the crunch.

In this Introduction we shall just look at the formalities of letter writing as they are transformed by Christian faith. You see, if you are really a Christian, everything you touch is done in a different way. You may do it in the same *form* as other people but the *content* will be different. Letter writing is a case in point. When a Christian writes a letter it is so different from other letters.

One of the first things a new secretary asked me was, "How do I do letters to So and So?" I had to say, "Well now, if it is a formal business letter, then this is how we write, but if it is to another Christian then it is going to be different – and this is the beginning and this is the end." When Christians are writing to each other, how different the letters are. Sometimes it even appears on the envelope. I get envelopes with "God loves you" written on the back. Or a text stuck on, or a sticker. Then I open it and it doesn't say "Dear Mr. Pawson...." It might say, "Dear brother in the Lord," and then it says, "Greetings in the Lord Jesus," and then some good news about the faith. A letter from a Christian is just so different from "Dear sir... Yours faithfully."

When Paul took over the form of letter writing which was normal in those days, he transformed every bit of it. In fact, he doubled up on everything. Instead of giving himself one authority, he gave himself two. Instead of giving one address he wrote two. Instead of giving one greeting, he gave two. It seems as if the Lord doubles the richness of life. Then, when Paul started saying nice things about them, he began to say it in threes. We shall find that the whole letter is so enriched in this way rather than being a mere formality. The opening verses could have been simply reading the outside of an envelope and of no value to us whatever. In fact, spiritual truth and the profound truths of the gospel come out even in the very first formalities.

The address is to God's nation; God's people. This is what somebody has called the third race, for that is what Christians are. Until Christ came there were only two races in the world: Jew and Gentile. But, when Christians came, a third race began – a new humanity. You belong to that race, that nation, if you are *in Christ*. This new nation had only been in existence for thirty years – *one new man in Christ*. For in Christ there is neither Jew nor Greek, bond nor free, male nor female, but all one in Christ. The third race was to be found in a little place in a valley now in eastern Turkey called Colossae.

He has never met them. They don't know his face, they

would not have recognised him if they passed him in the street. He has had no direct connection with this church, yet he is going to write to them and tell them what they must believe and how they must behave. He is going to offer these things not in the form of his advice or his opinion. He is going to tell them, "This is what you must believe and this is how you must behave," and he is going to say it in commanding terms. What authority has he to write such a letter to people he doesn't know?

The answer is very simple. Number one, he is an apostle of Jesus Christ. The word "apostle" there means something very strong. It is almost the word "ambassador". It means: I have his total authority and whatever I say, he will back up and therefore you are to accept my words as his. That is a very strong position to take. Secondly, he is saying that he did not choose this job, nor did man choose it for him, he got this job by the will of God. In fact, as we know from Paul's background, the very last thing he would have chosen to be, of all the careers open to him, was an apostle of Jesus Christ. In fact, he was in the early part of his life an apostle *against* Jesus Christ. His ambition was to destroy every follower of Jesus Christ. Yet on the Damascus road God met him. By God's choice, by God's will, he was an ambassador for Jesus for the rest of his life, and an ambassador to other nations than his own—to the Gentiles, to create a new third race, one man in Christ, one new humanity. So this is his authority: he is an apostle of Christ Jesus by the will of God. I don't think you can get much higher than that.

Imagine you had in your hand a certificate giving you the authority of the Queen. I had that when I became an officer in the Royal Air Force. That is nothing to the authority I have. Paul had a higher authority than I have. I am a teacher of Christ Jesus by the will of God, but he was an apostle of Christ Jesus by the will of God. He did not choose it, did not want it, did not earn it, did not achieve it—but God told him, and therefore he had the authority to tell someone else. He was under authority, therefore he had authority. Jesus himself was recognised by the Roman centurion as being one under authority, therefore having authority to say to someone else authoritatively: "That's what you must do."

Now I want to apply this very directly and frankly. One of the greatest causes of disunity in churches is an unwillingness to accept the authority of Paul. It is a division running right through ministers and clergy. It is not just among ministers and clergy, it is among Christians also who set the teaching of Paul over against the simple religion of Jesus and say, "Ah well, that's Paul," as much as to say, "That is only his opinion." Paul says, "My gospel is the only authoritative gospel and if anyone comes to you preaching another gospel, let him be anathema." He writes again in his letters, "I praise God that you accepted my words not as my opinion but as the word of the Lord." One of the biggest, perhaps the biggest division in the Christian Church today and among the churches is between those who say, "My religion is of Jesus and not of Paul," and those who say, "Paul's gospel is the gospel of our Lord Jesus Christ."

Let me bring this right down to earth. In the twentieth century a great debate arose in many churches on the position and function of women. It divided fellowships all over the place. I have read book after book by Christian leaders on the Christian liberation of women who write: "Ah, but that's only Paul." When Paul says the head of the woman is man and the head of man is Christ, that is what they say.

Into that situation comes this word, while in no way implying any difference in status or value whatever, he is describing *functioning within the body*. Paul says: "an apostle of Christ Jesus by the will of God". If you start picking and choosing what Paul says, and saying, "That is only Paul," then you are flying in the face of his claim to authority here—we cannot do it.

Take a more serious example: preaching on the wrath of God, as I have done. After preaching (as a visiting preacher) I was told in no uncertain terms by a bishop that it was the last time I would preach in that church. The reaction to preaching on the wrath of God was: "That is Paul, it is not the simple religion of Jesus." Paul says, "If you do not preach my gospel, if you have any other gospel than the one I have preached, then put a curse on that person." Here is an issue and it comes out in the first sentence of this epistle – strong meat.

Let me make it quite clear now, to be positive, I am willing to unite with anyone who will preach the gospel of Paul and have fellowship with them. I have been in a Roman Catholic presbytery with a Roman Catholic priest, and we spent two hours talking about the gospel of our Lord Jesus Christ, and we found that we believed the same gospel, and it was the gospel of Paul. God is doing surprising things today. He is showing where the truth really lies and it is sometimes in most unexpected places. The gospel is being preached more by the Roman Catholics in Europe today than in many free churches. It is the gospel that matters, and that is where it is working. That is where things happen and that is where blessings spread, as Paul says. That is where faith, hope and love are born. That is where lives are changed.

I would say this is going to be the touchstone among Christians. Do you recognise Paul as an apostle of Jesus Christ by the will of God, and do you accept his words as the word of the Lord? If you do, then brother give me your hand, we can have fellowship in grace and truth because there is only one gospel. As Paul says twice in these first eight verses, of the gospel as it really is: the gospel as truth and grace, which you heard from me, which you heard from

Epaphras, which must not be diluted. He cautions that you must not add to it, you must not subtract from it. It is in this gospel that you must stand firm, whatever it may cost.

That is where I personally stand. Unity must be a unity in the gospel. It will be the gospel that Paul preached as the apostle of Jesus. To those who preach that gospel, we should extend the hand of fellowship. Truth and grace are to be found in Paul's gospel.

Paul claims two commissions and he recalls two relationships. He keeps using the word "brother". The word "brother" usually has the family meaning: being a sibling. The word has also been used in a political connection and in the trades union movement. But in every other setting it is an exclusive word. There is one setting in which it is all-inclusive, so it is a synonym for "Christian". I wish it had never become a denominational label.

I read a book entitled *Born Again* which reduced me to tears. It told the story of the life of Charles Colson, the late President Nixon's hatchet man. It was said of him he would walk over his own grandmother to get what he wanted. He describes in his book how his ambition was to get into the heart of the corridors of power. He finished up in the Oval Office in the White House as Nixon's right-hand man, a member of the inner circle. At thirty-eight he had reached the pinnacle of his career. He describes how that whole administration slipped into a grey morality and then how it collapsed around his head. When it began to collapse, God touched Charles Colson and took him from the Oval Office down into a little room in the basement where a small group of senators met for prayer. There was a Jew there, a Roman Catholic and one other. He said, "Down in that basement I found out what brotherhood was, which I never found up in the Oval Office." He found men whose politics were totally opposite to his, praying for him. He found four men who were willing to go to prison instead of him so that he could stay with his wife and family. He would not let them do it, he went to prison himself. He had found men who were willing to lay down their lives for each other.

He had thought that he had been working for humanity, that he loved his country, and that the people in the Oval Office were brothers, but he discovered when the crash came that they were backbiting, jealous, fearful men, not brothers at all. He discovered brotherhood in the basement in a prayer meeting.

You have got to be born again to get into the family – if you are going to call someone "brother". You see, God has only one begotten Son, and therefore the idea of the brotherhood of man is a myth. It is a myth because God is not the Father of all men. You cannot be brothers until you have a common father. God has only one begotten Son, all the rest are adopted. But when you are adopted into God's family, when you are born again, then you can start saying, "Brother, sister," because you can start saying "Father". So Paul says: "To the brethren at Colossae." He has never seen them, never met them. He says, "Greetings from your brother Timothy," and I don't know if they have ever met Timothy. How is he able to call strangers "brother"? I'll tell you how—because he says, "Grace and peace to you from God the Father."

Have you not found this? I have found it again and again. I have met total strangers and within two minutes I feel I have known them for twenty years, and we are talking about things in common as if we were old buddies. We separate as if we had known each other for years. Anybody seeing us would have thought we were friends of years' standing. Why? Because we had a common Father before we met. Two relationships: brother; Father. You cannot have the horizontal without the vertical. When will mankind learn that you cannot be brothers until you have got the same Father?

Proof of this brotherhood is that Paul wrote a letter to a member of the church called Philemon, whose slave they called "useless" – Onesimus had run away to Rome. There in the big city he had found Paul in jail and had become a Christian. Paul sends him back, knowing that he could be crucified for being returned. But he sends the letter to Philemon. He is saying: Philemon, you can have your slave back, he is not useless now, you will find him useful now but you will find him more—you are receiving back a brother. He is your brother. That killed slavery – when your slave became not a tool, not some thing you bought, but someone to whom you were related. That is what was happening in the church at Colossae. Philemon and his slave sat at the same table and took bread and wine. They were now brothers. They would never have sat at the same table but for a common Father.

Paul gives his readers two titles. First, he calls them "saints". That word is so misleading now – unfortunately it seems to convey a sort of feel of outstanding piety, someone who is canonised. I wish the process of canonisation had never started because it implies that some, very few, Christians are saints. I believe in praying to the saints and what I mean by that is asking every Christian to pray for you. Because saints are not special people, you can meet them everywhere.

Saints are not necessarily people who are perfect. They are people on their way to being perfect, but they may still be a long way from it. A saint is somebody very special: someone who has been set apart from other people for God. He or she is one of God's people and that is what makes each saint special. God has drawn a distinction. Even if the church would not canonise someone, the Father does so for the sake of Jesus. You are a saint because you belong to him. The greatest distinction in the world is between saints and sinners. "Sinner" doesn't mean that somebody is worse than some of the saints, and "saint" doesn't mean that somebody is better than some of the sinners. A saint is someone who has been set apart for God and a sinner is someone who has not, and that is the first big distinction. Paul is addressing God's people in Colossae – his saints there. Everybody else is in the category of sinners, but you are saints. It means they have been set apart for God and therefore ought to be different, they ought to be better. But they are already saints and they are on their way to being better.

Among the saints Paul draws a further distinction. The first distinction is to separate the saints and the world. So he is declaring that the letter is not to sinners, it is to saints. Therefore, in a sense, there may be some reading this for whom this letter does not apply. It is not to you. If you get that feeling while we study it then I urge you to get among the saints as quickly as you can.

Then, among the saints Paul draws a second distinction: this letter is not even to all the saints, it is to the *faithful brothers*, and that is a smaller number still. We know already that there were some in the church who were not being faithful to the gospel but were drifting away into other things. So Paul makes his appeal to the faithful brethren, the reliable ones, the ones who stay with Christ. Every church relies for its continuity on the faithful brethren. You can have a lot of people moving in and out. Then you get the other sort, and you never know quite whether they will be still doing the job in a few weeks or whether they will have got upset and gone away. I thank God for the reliable brethren, the faithful brethren who say, "God has called me and I will stay, whatever the problems, whatever the difficulties, whatever the discouragements. You can always count on me being there. I'm not in and out." The faithful brethren hold the church. A church will vanish when you have lost your faithful brethren in it. They are the ballast that holds the ship upright and prevents shipwreck. You find out, as a church's fellowship goes on, who are the faithful brethren on whom you can rely. It is to those that Paul writes. He sees that this church could be shipwrecked. So he is saying: faithful brethren, I am writing to you that you may be rooted and grounded in him. There may also be those who read this letter and say, "I wonder if he would include me among the faithful brethren or just among the brethren. Am I one who helps to keep the church going or am I one of the unreliable ones?"

Now Paul attaches two addresses. Every Christian lives in two dimensions and has a dual citizenship. He or she belongs to the kingdom on earth and to the kingdom of heaven. One of the many tensions that come into a Christian's life is this one. You will have fewer tensions if you are not a Christian than if you are. When you become a Christian the tensions that come in your life are strong. There is the tension between the old life and the new for a start. There is the tension between being a citizen of the country in which you reside and a citizen of the kingdom of heaven—what a tension that is! So a Christian is often torn, and it is this dual life that we have to live until we get to heaven that is the source of much of our tension. Then there is tension between flesh and spirit. The tensions are there all right, and only the Holy Spirit can give us the victory.

So Paul includes two addresses. He says, "To the faithful brethren in Colossae; to God's people in Colossae." They have got to cope with the pettiness of that shrinking town. They have to cope with the commercial prosperity of it. They have to cope with the idolatry and immorality of it. They have to cope with the pagan atmosphere of it. They have to live in this city. They cannot get out of it, though some Christians love to go away and start a Christian community somewhere miles from anywhere where they can be just Christians. You are trying to anticipate heaven if you try to do that. God has placed you somewhere. But praise God that we also have another address: I live in Christ. One address is temporary; the other is permanent. One address is a horizontal address and the other is vertical: in Christ. One is an earthly address; the other is a heavenly address in heavenly places. We are all creatures of our environment, shaped by our surroundings. The question is: which of your addresses has most influence on you? You can live in Colossae (or somewhere else) and live a completely different life from the Colossians, provided "in Christ" is your real address.

Paul gives two greetings. He had a mixed background in that he was a Jew and he was a Roman citizen. He spoke Hebrew, he spoke Greek, and to a Gentile he would use Greek words *charis* and *eirene*. If he were speaking to Jews and using Hebrew he would say *shalom*, a lovely word which means peace, harmony of body, mind, spirit, family.

In Christ such words cease to be wishes and they become realities—grace and peace to you. So a Christian does not *wish* things on other people, but *pronounces* them on other people. At the end of a service that I take I do not *wish* the benediction, I *pronounce* it. I would not say, "I hope you have the grace of the Lord Jesus; I hope you find a bit of the love of God and I hope maybe you'll have a bit of the Holy Spirit this week." Can you imagine a minister finishing a service like that? In Christ, the greetings become certainties and you are able to say, "The grace of the Lord Jesus Christ and the love of God and the fellowship of the Holy Spirit be with you." It is pronounced. So Paul does not just say: I hope you will be happy, harmonious and healthy. He says, "Grace and peace to you," because they are in Christ as well as in Colossae so he can pronounce it.

Paul then moves from greetings to gratitude. We have noted that it was usual to say something nice about people, especially before you were going to say something nasty. It was also the custom, as it still is in many letters, to have something at the beginning that cheered people up – at worst a bit of flattery, at best a compliment or a congratulation, and that is as far as the world can go. So some letters in the world flatter the recipient, or they compliment them or they congratulate them, making them feel good. Paul never descended to that level. For one thing, Paul always said, "I congratulate *God* on what you are. I compliment *God* for you. I thank *God* whenever I pray for you." If God had done something, Paul gave glory to him.

So instead of congratulations or compliments he says: "I thank God for your faith, for your hope, for your love." So, once again, an ordinary letter is transformed because a Christian is writing not a merely human congratulation or compliment but a form of praise to God. "I thank God...." It is a very delicate balance here—we should thank each other, but behind all service that we recognise in the church we should be very careful that we don't descend to the level of a mere human club or society and pass votes of thanks at church meetings to someone who has taken the collection for fifty-seven years. We should thank the Lord for their fidelity, for their love. Praise him, it is his work, not theirs. Glory where glory is due – to God. But for the grace of God, they would not have done that thing. But for the glory and grace of God, they would never have been faithful through those years. So Paul looks up and says, "Whenever I pray and I think about you, I thank God for you and I praise God for you."

What does he praise God for? He thanks God for the *gospel*. The good news, the gospel, is the heart of the matter. Paul is saying: I praise God for the good news and the effect it has had on you. He mentions three fruits of the gospel: faith, hope and love. Have you realised that those three things constantly come together in the Bible? Most people know 1 Corinthians 13: "Now abides faith, hope, and love; and the greatest of these is love." Did you know it came in 1 Thessalonians? Do you know that the other apostles always put them together? Faith, hope, love, these are the three tests as to whether the gospel as it truly is has been preached, for those three things result. Not: "Do you get a lot of people here?" Not: "Do you get big collections?" Not: "Do you have a full programme of many activities?"

The real tests of a church are these: Are people growing in faith? Are they tackling bigger things than they tackled a few years ago? Are they believing more or less? Is their hope strengthening? Are they living more and more in the future and looking forward more and more to what God has for them? Are they more loving with each other than they were? Are they closer to each other than they were? If a church passes those tests then I will tell you the gospel is being preached in it by someone. The gospel as it really is has been proclaimed because that is what happens. So Paul thanks God for their faith in Jesus.

You are exercising faith every day. You cannot live without faith. When I step on a bus I am exercising faith in the bus driver. When I get on a plane I am exercising even more faith in the pilot. When I go into a hospital I am putting faith in the surgeon. You cannot live without faith. When I write a cheque or put my money in a bank, I am putting faith in my bank manager that he will look after it. Every minute of every day I am putting faith in someone or something. But the faith that the gospel produces is that same kind of trust in Jesus, so that people trust him increasingly for what they need.

Now let me make it absolutely clear that faith is not something you do with your head. Faith is not accepting the truth of what I say from a pulpit; faith is acting on the Word of God. One of the most misleading translations there ever was appeared in most English Bibles: "Faith without works is dead." That made people think that you have to add good deeds to faith. It does not mean that at all. J. B. Phillips and the Good News Bible have got it right: "Faith without action is dead." In other words, if faith is all in your head and you never act on it – you never actually *trust* Jesus – it is not faith. Faith is what you *do*, not what you *think*.

You know, the devil could recite the Apostles' Creed from beginning to end. "I believe in God the Father Almighty, Maker of heaven and earth...." So does Satan. He trembles about it, but he does not put his faith in Jesus. Most preachers use the well-known illustration of Charles Blondin and Niagara Falls. Blondin, the tightrope walker put a tightrope across Niagara Falls from the Canadian to the American bank. He walked right across with a sixteen-foot balancing pole. When he got to the other side he threw it away and walked right back without the pole and the crowds cheered. Then he got a wheelbarrow with a hollow rim wheel and wheeled it right across the wire. Then he put a sack of potatoes in it and wheeled it right back across Niagara Falls. Finally, he said to a titled English gentleman, "Do you believe that I could take a man across in this barrel?" That Englishman said, "Yes, I believe that you could. I think the Duke of Newcastle would be a very suitable person." The Duke declined. But Blondin's mother got into the barrel and he took his mother across. Now who believed in Blondin?

I don't care if you sing hymns about Jesus or recite the Apostles' Creed—you could teach a budgerigar to do that. It is when you actually step out in faith and rely on the Lord Jesus and put yourself in a position where you are going to look an absolute fool, and come to an awful crash if he is not there—that is when you have faith in Jesus Christ. It is when a church is willing to accept impossible targets and say,

"We believe in Jesus." Set no targets and it is comfortable because you will never fail. Every act of faith is the statement of a target. Every goal is a statement of faith.

Paul thanks God for their faith in Jesus. Now faith, if it is faith in Jesus, will very quickly lead to another by-product. As soon as you really believe in Jesus you find someone alongside you who also believes in Jesus and you love them. Faith labours in love and this new dimension comes. Paul goes on and praises him for their love for all the saints. Notice the little word *all*. If you love *some* of the saints then that is not Christian love. That is no more than you can manage in ordinary human society. If a church is simply a loose connection of cliques, that is not love—love for all the saints means love for all the saints, no more, no less. Love for all the saints means love for those you would normally not talk to, love for those who are not your social type, love for those you don't really know how to relate to because they are so different from you.

You try it after a Sunday morning service and see how you get on. Go to someone who isn't your type, who isn't your age, who isn't your background, and just see. If you are both believers in Jesus you will find love begins to flow between you. So I thank God for your faith in Jesus, for your love for all the saints and that doesn't just mean all of them in the local church; it means all of them all over the world and that will be shown in so many ways. It will be shown by writing to people you have never met or seen. It will be shown by praying for Christians in prison. Love for all the saints is the second fruit of the gospel.

Then Paul teaches how you, the believers, got the faith and the love. Faith and love are based on hope. Now I wonder if you ever realised that if you are a believer and if you have begun to love your fellow believers, it all started with hope. That is the fundamental virtue. Hope begins the process.

Why? Because it is hope that introduces the dimension of another world to you. It is as soon as you really realise there is a heaven and that there is a possibility of your getting there that you begin to believe and you then begin to love. You see, if there is no heaven, why believe? It is because you began to understand that there is a heaven and that Jesus could get you there that you began to believe in Jesus. Why do you begin to love other people or seek to love them? It is because you are going to live with them in heaven, you might as well get to know them now, learn how to live with them here, and have a foretaste of heaven as you do so. Your hope is the key to the other things.

In the book of Ecclesiastes, the reason why that man seems to have so little faith and so little love is precisely because he has no hope, because he says, "Who knows what will happen to me when I die." When you ask that question and cut the nerve of hope, then frankly there is no point in faith, no point in love. The only thing you can do is what Ecclesiastes describes—eat, drink, and enjoy what you have earned. That is what most people do, because what point is there in doing anything else if you have no hope of anything beyond the grave? But Paul teaches: I thank God for your faith in Jesus and your love for all the saints, which are based on your hope in heaven, which is kept there for you. Frankly, that is the best place to invest. The only place you can keep anything without it being corroded is in heaven. How good is your bank account up there at the moment? Have you ever thought? Have you asked for a statement? Why not do that and say, "Lord, give me a statement as to how my account stands up there." For Jesus told you to lay up treasure there. He told you how to do it as well. I tell you now that neither moth nor rust can consume, nor inflation nor devaluation touch your treasure there. What an offer! I feel like putting a whole page advertisement in the *Financial Times*: "Greatest investment offer ever! No deflation, no devaluation. A hope kept securely in heaven for you." The phrase "kept securely" Paul took straight from the stock exchange of his day; it is a financial word. So if you think I am pushing it, I am just expounding the Word of God.

Paul lists three links. Remember that it had only been thirty years since Jesus had died when the apostle wrote this letter, yet the gospel had spread from Jerusalem to Rome. Already it had gone to places to which Paul had never been, permeating the whole world. Little did Paul know that even an emperor would become a Christian in the foreseeable future. Paul himself was talking of taking the gospel to Spain, and this was within thirty years, so how does the gospel spread like that?

We have been thanking God for the fruit of the gospel with Paul. We now thank God for the furtherance of the gospel. We know what the fruit is, but what explains the furtherance of the gospel? Today we could ask what explains the fact that the church is growing faster today than it has grown for two thousand years. What explains the fact that the gospel is permeating into every country throughout the world? What are the links in the chain? Well, there are three answers Paul gives.

First of all, the gospel spreads by itself. It has life within it—it is the living Word; it is the living gospel, dynamite (Greek: *dunamis*). The gospel can blow a man apart and put him together again. It can turn the world upside down; it can blow a situation to bits. Paul is teaching that the first reason why the gospel is spreading so rapidly, through Colossae, and up and down the valley to Laodicea and other places: because it is alive; it is dynamite.

There is a big condition: *provided* it is preached as the gospel that is really true—the gospel as it really is. Now that is why it is not dynamite in some places, because it has been watered down. It comes as human opinion instead of divine authority, and then it is not dynamite. But the true gospel is. It has within it the capacity to spread and grow. It is like a seed. You put a little seed in the ground and it looks so lifeless, but it has that within it which can grow and spread and bring fruit. The word of the gospel is that kind of a word – it does not return to God void. It has life in it; it is sharp and quick—it is *active*. That is the first reason. It therefore grows in quality and quantity, spreading and fruiting as Paul says. A church that is not growing in quantity and quality is a church that has lost the gospel.

I praise God that some believers don't just sit and listen on Sundays but go and share with someone else what they have heard. When you do that, you find that people come to your home—they want to know, they are prepared to listen. You can have neighbours in your home and take the gospel, take the Bible and explain it to them. You find that they are interested, they are hungry; they want to know. If only all were doing that and not just listening to it. If you are preaching the gospel, you find that you have got "dynamite" too. You don't need to have a big congregation to preach.

There is a text in Acts 8 which touches me. "Philip preached unto him Jesus" – a congregation of one, but he passed the gospel on and it was dynamite and it changed that man's life. Have you got a congregation of one? Ten? I tell you this: if you preach the gospel you will soon have a bigger one. You will soon find if you give them the word of truth, of grace, that there will be more wanting to hear, as Charles Colson did when he went into prison. His description of prison is pretty rough, a situation in which he did not quite know what to do. But within just a very short while he had four people meeting for prayer and gradually it spread through that prison, and the word of life set men free in prison. He writes, "The Lord had to put me in jail to set me free." There were people in that jail more free than people walking around the streets and on the subway. So it has got the power within itself.

The second thing, which we have already been thinking about, is that the power of the gospel only works when it has a human channel willing to *speak* it. Now of course you do have to *live* it as well or your words won't be listened to. But it is a half-truth to say, "We are only called to live it." We are not all called to be evangelists, and that needs to be made clear. But if you want to discover the power of the gospel you have got to be willing to let your mouth be used. It is only as you speak it that its power is released.

As you live it, its power is not released, but as you speak it the very words take life and things happen, and faith, hope, and love are born in other people. So what God is looking down from heaven for, and waiting for in this country, are churches throughout this land with no silent saints among them, but people who are able to give a reason, to speak, who will say: "I know whom I have believed, therefore I speak," and when they speak, things happen. So Paul is teaching that the gospel is spreading because it is alive itself but it has spread because a man called Epaphras came on our behalf to you and told you the truth.

So we are looking for mouths. Deliver us, Lord, from "lockjaw" – set us speaking the truth. There is no reason not to. If you can talk about the weather you can talk about Jesus. If you can talk about the prices in the supermarket, you can talk about Jesus. You might feel some embarrassment and think that other things need dealing with first. But if you can talk at all, you can talk about Jesus, surely. So God is wanting preachers not just in pulpits but in the shop and the office, when the occasion occurs. I would say quite frankly for myself, and I think it to be true of most Christians, that it is not occasions for speaking about Christ that we lack, it is courage. Is that not true? When you look back, you know you have missed time after time when you could have said a word. Afterwards you knew that with just a little bit of guts you could have said something. Like the man in the factory toilet who heard someone say "Christ" when something happened. He just turned to him and said, "Would you mind? You're talking about my best friend." Just a word, but it got through. That other man never again used the word "Christ" like that.

Finally, the third factor in the communication of the gospel is that a network of communication is set up by the Spirit; a spiritual bond. This is what surprised Charles Colson. As soon as he became a Christian he found himself part of a network. He found letters coming to him from all over America. He found people saying, "I'm praying for you." Paul says, "Epaphras has come to Rome to tell me of the love the Spirit has given you" – and that is the network. Good news spreads quickly, like a prairie fire. C. S. Lewis called Christianity a "healthy infection". It is the only healthy infection I know in the world. Health is not normally infectious; it is disease that is infectious. It is as often caught as taught. It spreads because human beings talk and because the Spirit creates a bond in which we like to hear, in which we want to know, in which people say, "I have heard of this happening over there and that happening over there" – and we get to know. People think Christians live a narrow life, but we have a wider social contact. You hear more of what is going on; you become part of a network of communication, of love in the Spirit around the world and you do not know where it is going to lead next.

Read Colossians 1:1 – 29

When I prepare a talk on the Bible, what I do is to read the passage repeatedly until I begin to *feel* it. Not many people go for the emotions, but the Bible is written in a very emotional way and it is full of deep feelings, so I read a passage until I have got the feelings. There may be feelings of surprise, delight or whatever, but I need to get the feel of a passage before I speak on it.

Somebody once asked me what was my favourite book in the Bible and I replied, honestly, "It's the last one I've studied". Therefore, at the time of writing, Colossians is my favourite book in the Bible. But it is not the most popular book in the Bible by a long way – but I hope it will be by the time we have finished this study.

We look, first of all, at Colossae. Does the letter tell us anything about the place? Then we are going to look at the church in Colossae of which some wonderful things are said. Then we want to look at Paul (or Saul) and his commitment to the church even though he has never been there. That is the first big surprise of this letter. It is one of the very few letters Paul wrote to a church he had never been to, and he would need to have had a very good reason for writing to complete strangers. Then I want us to look at Christ himself: why did Paul have such a remarkable view of our Lord?

So let us start very simply. Where is Colossae, and for what is it famous? The answer is: nothing. It is up the

Meander River from Ephesus where the river meets the sea, and the river meanders right through the country, and that is why we get the word "meandering". Way up at the head of that river was a little cluster of towns that included Laodicea and Colossae. Each of those little towns had a church in it and they were flourishing, especially the church at Colossae. I do not know what the name means. It has a kind of subtle feel of something very big in this town, something colossal. But that applies to another town down in Crete, so I cannot tell you that it is named after some colossal mountain, monument or such like. But it was a colossal church and to us that is what it was famous for.

Paul had nothing to do with that, but he did have an indirect contact because that church was founded by a man called Epaphras, one of Paul's converts, who had occupied a role towards this church which Paul did not have. Epaphras was already such a convert of Paul that he was starting his own churches and Paul rejoiced in those churches. He was not the father of the church but he was the "grandfather", in that Epaphras was his "son in the gospel". The church that Epaphras had started already had a really good reputation in that area. For what? For faith, hope and love – and that is a pretty good reputation to have. So Paul could write to them as his grandchildren and that is why he could claim some authority over them, and that is why he could write to them with a strong word, which we will look at.

There is nothing else to say about the place; but there is more that can be said about the church there. Successful evangelism by Epaphras had left a lovely church. One of the biggest problems today for Christians is to find a church where we can happily fit in, but we would all have fitted in happily to the church at Colossae. It was running on the right lines from the very beginning.

Let us ask now: what was Paul doing, writing to them?

What is the letter about? We have to ask what it was that was alarming Paul about what was happening. He was concerned about the danger they were in. It is a very widespread danger today. Paul heard about something and he immediately put that church on his prayer list, and his team were not involved in the church in any way other than prayer, on the good principle that if you cannot preach to people, you can pray for them. He and his team (which included Timothy) were prayer partners already with this church and had been for some years. Furthermore, it had cost them. They had struggled and suffered because they prayed for this church, and Paul says, making a rather unusual point, that he did not feel he had suffered enough for them. He had in his mind a kind of target of suffering: as much as Christ suffered for them, and he said that he was still short of making up his sufferings in his body for this church. So for many years they prayed and they tell us exactly what they prayed. They prayed for their knowledge, for their power and above all, for their stickability (my own word). It was Paul's concern that they never shifted from where they had started. He was concerned that clever-sounding arguments were attacking that stability and were being adopted by some of the members of the church. We see more about that in chapter 2.

What were the wrong things being taught? They were on the main road from Europe to Asia and all the latest philosophies and ideas passed through there. It was a whole mix of speakers who, with very clever-sounding arguments, were introducing dangerous ideas to the church, which could eventually destroy this very successful fellowship.

I do not need to tell you about Paul, the writer. You have probably heard so much about him that you know everything about him that I know. So there is nothing to tell you, except that his conversion did everything for him here. In that conversion experience, all of Paul's basic theology, all his basic ideas, were formed. We can recall the heart of the experience. He had been on his way to Damascus to imprison Christians and shut up the gospel. He was therefore an anti-Christian missionary before ever he said anything for Christ. Suddenly, at the foot of Mount Hermon, that snow-covered peak in the north, a light shone on him which was so bright that he knew it must be heaven, and he was brought up short by this light, he was blinded by it, and he would have to be healed of his blindness by a Christian in Damascus. Out of that, his question was: Who are you, Lord, that you are shining on me like this?

The answer came: I am Jesus of Nazareth whom you are persecuting. Immediately, in that reply, all Paul's theology came in, now that he knew that Jesus was alive and that Jesus of Nazareth could be persecuted by persecuting his church – and therefore the church must be his body on earth. Suddenly, you can see how Paul's ideas came barging through into his mind and they were all correct theology. He got it right from the start. What we want to look at now is the most important thing. For Paul, Christianity was Christ. It is as simple as that. If you had Christ, you were a Christian. If you did not have Christ, you were not. It is simple. But he called Jesus of Nazareth Christ, and he constantly calls him Christ, and he calls him something else. He calls him "Lord". That is a mark of a true Christian. If they say "the Lord Jesus Christ", you know they are a true Christian. Plenty of people talk about Jesus. Plenty talk about Jesus Christ, but they have no idea why they call him Christ. Many think that it is just a kind of surname that Jesus picked up on the way. But only where somebody calls him "the Lord Jesus Christ" has he found the true faith that saves him. We want to look at those three words. We know what "Jesus" meant. It talks about a Galilean carpenter who for most of his life worked in that little town of Nazareth that he became attached to and known by, and for all his time on earth he was called "Jesus of Nazareth" – the name he was given by his parents plus the address of his birth certificate, if you like.

But here is the most important question in this part of our study. When and why did Christians start to call Jesus of Nazareth "our Lord Jesus Christ"? Those are important titles. They have each had a history; they have each embodied certain things that could be believed about a person. I find myself looking at those little words now: our Lord Jesus Christ. The funny thing is that at one stage in the history of Christ, those two titles were attached to him by God the Father. When Peter preached the first Christian sermon on the day of Pentecost, he finished with these words. At the very end of his sermon, Peter showed that he was a true Christian. You know roughly how Peter preached on the day of Pentecost; he talked about Jesus all the way through, but he finished his sermon with this sentence: "Therefore, let all Israel be assured of this. God has made this Jesus whom you crucified both Lord and Christ." You find that the other early Christians had all adopted this understanding of Jesus of Nazareth. He is now Lord and Christ and they talk about our Lord Jesus Christ. It became the test as to whether they had found a Christian; if a person would say those three words, he was a Christian.

When did they all suddenly find that Jesus of Nazareth had these two titles that God the Father gave his Son? It was after his resurrection and before he gave the gift of the Holy Spirit, and they all learned to use these titles. It came to me very forcibly as I thought about these words for this study, that there were two facts of history which had happened, which God used in this.

The first event was the resurrection and that unique event was proved to them by the risen Jesus. That historic event caused them to reverse all that they were thinking about the cross. It changed their whole understanding of the cross that Jesus faced. And they realised – and this is the important thing – that Jesus chose to die, that he was in charge of it all. He chose when to die, where to die, how to die and he had arranged the whole thing, and they saw this so clearly now through the resurrection. They realised Jesus had known what he was doing all the time and that he was not a victim of injustice but was the victor – he had arranged it and he was in charge of it. That, in itself, is a revolution in thinking, because on the day that Jesus died, their hopes in him had been shattered. When he talked to two of them on the road to Emmaus, they were very disappointed in Jesus, and they said: we hoped that he would redeem Israel; we hoped all this. When all your hopes have been centred on someone and he is then put to a criminal death of extreme pain, shame and loneliness.... Yet all the time, he was in charge, and he had chosen all this. That is why there are so many references to the cross in the introduction here – to the way Jesus chose to die. That is the first historical act which determined the word Lord.

But what brought about the word Christ? Well, the answer is that, just a few weeks after the resurrection, the ascension happened and they saw him go to heaven and therefore, they now changed their view of his birth because they realised he chose to be born. Now there are the two great shifts in their understanding of Jesus of Nazareth: first, that he chose to die; second, that he chose to be born. He never said, "I was born"; he always said, I came – which was unique. He said: I came to do this; I came to find those who were lost; I came to look for the lost. Another person might have said: I was born to do this. But he said that he came to do this, and he said, no man has been up to heaven except the Son of Man who is in heaven. It is an amazing statement.

So there was a totally new understanding of Jesus: that he

had come from heaven, from the very place where God had his throne. Therefore, you have a totally new perspective on Jesus of Nazareth from those two events which gave us the two titles Lord and Christ. Of the two, Christ was the favourite one of the writer of this letter. If you go through it and underline "Christ", that comes up again and again in Colossians.

Paul now talks about the *mystery* of Christ. That word does not mean that it is mysterious or that there is something not quite normal about it. It is totally abnormal actually. The word "mystery" needs to be understood. In scripture, the word always means a secret that has been held for centuries which, at last now, is being told openly. The secret was "Christ in you, the hope of Glory" and so we now know the secret, we now know the mystery of Christ and it has been told to us. And we can share the mystery. The secret can now be told. That is what the early apostles said when they preached the gospel and I think that is very exciting. It has been my job for years to share that secret with people and, as I did so, it was sheer joy to share the secret of our Lord Jesus Christ, the secret that can now be told. And Paul is determined to tell it. He describes in this passage how he was commissioned and how he was called by Jesus himself who told him to go and tell the Gentiles the secret – which he did. The secret was Christ in you. Christ in the Gentiles. Now "Christ" was a Jewish word and it means so much to the Jews. It meant the coming King, the King like David they had waited for – for centuries. He had come, and they could now tell others he had come. It was said at his birth, when the wise men said, "Where is he that is born King of the Jews?" And it was the secret told at his death when Pontius Pilate had a lapse of conscience and put "King of the Jews" on the cross above his head and in the known languages. It is very exciting to be one who can tell secrets. But that word

Christ meant the highest possible position. It is a heavenly title. Jesus is the supreme Being. That is something very precious, but it is something very startling, if you just for a moment stop and consider that we now believe that Jesus of Nazareth is the Christ. That is our faith and that means Jesus the Messiah and everything the "Messiah" means to the Jew, we now know Jesus is. I want to shout "Hallelujah!"

The one word that stuck out, for me, in the middle of chapter 1 was that he might be the supremacy. That is a unique word only found in this little letter: that Jesus is the Supremacy and that is what he is to us, too.

We of course did not have the historic experiences of the resurrection or the ascension, but we have believed the testimony of those who did have it. And because we believe the testimony of those people, those two events are very precious to us – regarding the supremacy of Jesus. By him, all things were made, and all things were made by him and for him. What a remarkable statement. The carpenter of Nazareth, before he made chairs and tables, made the wood from which they come. And before he preached the Sermon on the Mount, and other sermons, he made the mountains. In those first few verses – from chapter 1:10 to v. 20 – there is a list of titles and positions. Jesus is the head of the Body, and not just all things were made by him, but all powers, all rulers, all authorities were created by him and for him. That is what comforted the early Christians when they paid the supreme penalty for believing this. You died for that faith. You died if you believed such a thing.

You can understand now how quickly Christians were accused of being traitors to Rome. They had their own King now and that is the basic cause of the persecution that broke out quite quickly against the early church. We have another King, and to proclaim that everywhere, against all other authorities, all other kingships, was to be a "traitor", and to pay for such "treachery" with your life.

What is your reaction to these opening verses? It is an astonishing faith: to believe that a village carpenter from ancient days is in charge of all authorities, all powers on earth, because he made them all. They were made by him and for him. Dare you believe it? It is so easy for somebody to say: you don't believe that, do you? It is so easy to criticise that as a statement of faith but in fact it is there in those few verses 1:10–20.

Above all, he is the image of the invisible God. It pleased God that all his "Godness" – I will put it that way – is seen in Christ. Therefore, if you have got Christ, that will give you amazing courage when people criticise, and amazing confidence in your faith.

All that is just the introduction, which is really exciting. And we have not even dug into the important teaching of the epistle which Paul is trying to avoid until later.

Now please read the rest of Colossians 2 (from verse 6 to the end of the chapter) because that is what it is all about and what they are in danger of losing. If anything starts replacing Christ in a church, they are in danger of dying. Nothing must replace Christ. That is what the word means. He is the indispensable head of the Church, and as soon as anybody else tries to be head of the church, be it a pope or anyone else, you are going to lose the essence of the church.

Read Colossians 2:1–5

Our theme in this passage is *knowing* Christ – the knowledge we need, the convictions we need. Before we can know more about him we have got to admit that we don't know enough. We live in an age which glorifies agnosticism. If you want to be respected intellectually you must put yourself among the "don't knows". The more we discover with our science the more we realise that we know very little indeed. Even scientific theories that were taught to us in school as hard fact are now being revised in the light of new discoveries. Those who thought they understood how all the stars in the heavens worked discovered black holes and were thrown into real uncertainties about the universe. The result is that anybody who says, "I know" is regarded with suspicion. At best they are thought to be eccentric and at worst fanatical. To say "I know something" is regarded as intellectual pride. It is setting yourself up above other people and saying, "I know better than you. I have greater intellect than you. I've discovered something you haven't." That makes it the more embarrassing to be a Christian these days.

Those of us who go into schools and colleges and speak for the Lord, very quickly come up against young people who in discussion afterwards challenge this "I know" and say, "How do you know and what right do you have to say that you know when everybody else is humble enough to admit that they know very little?" Even science is taking on a humbler aspect than it once did. Yet a Christian is someone who knows. A Christian is someone who says "I know the truth." I remember hearing of a Christian who was asked, "Do you think you have the truth?" That Christian just replied quite simply and sincerely, "No, but the truth has me" – and this sounds offensive to some.

We are going to look at the mental side of Christianity. It is not a side that moves you deeply in your emotions and unfortunately this mental assurance – this conviction of knowing what you believe and whom you believe – is also under attack from within the Church. It is being attacked by those who feel that head knowledge has no part in Christian assurance and that in fact Christian assurance comes from feelings rather than from facts – those who would judge a service or a sermon by what emotions have taken place in their heart as they have gone through the service.

But there is a place for thinking. There is a place for loving God with your mind. There is a place for thinking through what you believe so that you are able to give a reason to everyone who asks you concerning the hope that is in you. There is a place for studying to show yourself approved by God, rightly handling the Word of truth. There is a place for thinking in Christian assurance.

In the first five verses of Colossians 2, Paul is talking about the mental part of being a Christian. Later he will move on to the moral side, but I warn you now that you are quite unlikely to have any feelings at all during this study. Maybe God will give us a bonus, but we are going to think hard. Paul is still being very personal. He is talking about his own ministry. He says, "I want you to realise how I agonise for you Christians whom I have never met personally." Suddenly a window is opened into Paul, which shows us a very remarkable feature. Most of us find that we can be concerned about Christians we have met. We find it very difficult to be deeply concerned about Christians we have never known personally. To agonise for people you don't know – even though you are involved in a great struggle with them – is not easy.

I was reading again a passage where Paul describes some of the real burdens that he carried in life. Think about this list of things he went through and particularly the one that climaxes the list, that caps it all. He says, "I have served more prison sentences than others; I have been beaten times without number; I have faced death again and again; I have been beaten the regulation thirty-nine stripes by the Jews five times; I have been beaten with rods three times; I have been stoned once; I have been shipwrecked three times; I have been twenty-four hours in the open sea. In my travels I have been in constant danger from rivers and floods, from bandits, from my own countrymen, and from pagans. I have faced danger in city streets, danger in the desert, danger on the high seas, danger among false Christians. I have known exhaustion, pain, long vigils, hunger, and thirst, doing without meals, cold and lack of clothing." Now what would you say could be worse than all that? "And apart from all these trials I have the daily responsibility for all the churches," as much as to say that is the greatest agony of them all. "Do you think anyone is weak without my feeling his weakness? Does anyone have his faith upset without my longing to restore him?" Do you feel the heart of Paul there? This is the agony, which he is describing to the Colossians. He has never met them, and he has never been to their church, but he has heard that their faith is being upset. So he literally says, "I want you to know how I agonise for you." The Greek word he uses is *agon* from which we get our word "agony". He says, "When I heard that your faith is being upset, all of me was in pain. I long to restore you and all the shipwrecks, and the stonings, and the beatings are nothing compared to the agony of seeing a Christian's faith upset."

When he agonised in that way, he always did something about it. When he thought about them and agonised for them, he would pray for them, he would write to them. He would send someone to them; he would do something to get them back on to an even keel, to get them back on to a firm foundation. He would do it for churches he had never been to, churches he had not founded, converts who had been won by someone else.

Here beats the heart of a true evangelist. Here is an evangelist who is not only concerned to bring people to faith but to see that they remain in that faith. Here is an evangelist who not only starts people on the Christian road and then pushes off somewhere else, but an evangelist who agonises over his concerns that those he has started go on and get built up in the faith.

In eighteenth-century England, there were two great evangelists wandering around. Three really, but two were brothers and did their work together so we will treat them as one. There were two great evangelistic crusades going on. One man was called George Whitefield, and my, that man really could preach. He won thousands of people for the Lord. When he brought people to the Lord he moved on somewhere else and he preached and brought hundreds more to the Lord. In those days, England had two great evangelistic crusades going on all the time, and the other was run by the Wesley brothers John and Charles. John Wesley led thousands to the Lord but, and this was the great difference, John Wesley and his brother Charles went back to the converts and built them into little cells of twelve, which they called "class meetings" – to larger families, which they called "societies", and they established a structure that built up people in the faith, and Charles Wesley wrote hymns for them to sing – hymns like "And Can It Be" and "O For a

Thousand Tongues to Sing". He wrote six thousand hymns for Christians, to build them up in the faith and give them a strong foundation so that they knew what they believed because they had sung it so often.

At the end of George Whitefield's life, Whitefield wrote to Wesley, and though Whitefield had seen more conversions, Whitefield said to Wesley, "My work is a rope of sand. You have built them up. You've conserved them. You've made sure." Now that is true evangelism. Wesley was a Paul kind of evangelist. When Paul heard of a Christian whose faith was being upset, he was in more agony than if he was beaten with rods. He longed to restore them and he wanted to do something about it. So at this point his words mean: I have never met you; I've never been to your church; I don't know you personally and I don't know the people at Laodicea twelve miles down the valley either – but I know your faith has been upset and I am longing to help you and I am writing because I don't want you to be upset: I want you not only to have faith; I want you to have a strong faith and a clear faith. I want you to know what you believe. I want you to be filled with wisdom and knowledge and understanding. I want you to have the courage of your convictions. I want you to be knit together in love. I want you to have the full assurance that understanding brings.

Do you get his ambition coming through – his general aim? His aim for all his converts was that their faith would be strong enough so that it was unshakeable, and that no matter who argued with them, they could not shake that person. Now that should be the ambition of every true evangelist and preacher and pastor. He wanted to make his people so strong in the faith and clear in the faith that the most brilliant arguer would not be able to shake them, so that the most reasonable logical and persuasive argument could do nothing to move them from where they stood. Indeed, that is the point of having a strong teaching ministry.

I used to rejoice in a church I pastored that the Jehovah's Witnesses and the Mormons and other visitors soon found out that they didn't stand much chance if somebody said, "I go to that church." I was glad about that because however persuasive the arguments may have sounded, and however much it might have seemed like Christian truth was being offered, members knew what they believed and the arguments didn't shift them. That was my ambition for the congregation, that they should be quite clear in their minds and know the fundamentals of the faith so that nobody could move them and they could not have that faith upset.

You need certain things to complement your faith. First of all, *courage*. It is one thing to know what you believe, it is another thing to have the courage to say so. It is another thing to have the courage to be outspoken about it, to say, "Well I don't care how you argue. This is what I believe and I don't care if you know it." This is a day, as I have pointed out, when we could be tempted to be ashamed or embarrassed because we can say "I know." People will think we are being conceited when we say that, but we must not be ashamed. We must have the courage to say, "I do know." It requires courage in such an agnostic era to state that. So Paul says, "I pray that you would have the complement of courage to your faith." That you may have the courage of your convictions – not just have convictions but have courage.

Secondly, what a help it is to stand for your faith and to be outspoken about it if you know that behind you is a loving *fellowship* in which you are welded together with others who also know what you know. Too often, Christians have been knocked down because they have stood and been attacked alone, and they have not had the strength of knowing that whilst they may be alone in the workplace, behind them there is a fellowship and they are knitted together in love with them. That makes you strong in your faith. So Paul says, "I pray that you may be filled with courage to make your faith strong. I pray that you may be knit together." The word is literally ligaments and tendons, and love is the ligament of Christian fellowship.

Thirdly, Christians are going to need to have full assurance and it is not going to be good enough for them to say, "Well, I think that this is so." If there is one phrase I can't stand hearing preachers use it is, "I venture to suggest." We are not venturing to suggest, we are saying, "I know whom I have believed" – with full assurance, with confidence. So here are three things we need to complement our faith: courage, the backing of a loving fellowship, and full assurance. Now how does all that come? The answer is that it comes through understanding. If you don't understand, you cannot have those three things.

I am intrigued now about the content of the faith. There are three words used here: knowledge, wisdom, and understanding. You are going to need those three dimensions in your head if you are going to be able to speak with full assurance. Wisdom means being able to grasp the truth; knowledge means being able to present the truth, and understanding means being able to apply the truth. Christian truth is composed of these three dimensions. Those who can make a strong witness are those who can grasp the truth, present the truth and apply the truth, and those are three quite different things. To grasp the truth is to say, "I see. I understand. I have apprehended the truth." To be able to present the truth means to be able to present it clearly and intelligibly so that people understand what you are saying and what you believe. To apply the truth is to be able to say, "In this situation, this is how the truth applies. This is what you need to do as the result of the truth." Now does that sound like a pretty tall order – that every Christian should be able to grasp the truth, present the truth, and apply the truth? Why that's going to mean we will all have to head off for a theological seminary; we are all going to have to get a degree; we are all going to have to read book after book after book. We are not all capable of doing that. Surely it is only a few who can do this. Well, I have good news for you. The good news is that there is a secret, a bit of a shortcut to all three, and the secret is Christ. This is the great secret of God: that if you want to be able to grasp the truth, if you want to be able to present the truth, if you want to be able to apply the truth, then there is only one thing you need to know, or rather it is one person—Christ. Now we have a remarkable picture in our minds. Paul uses picture language at this point.

I want you to picture a treasure chest, bound with metal. It is a strong chest and you cannot break into it or force it. There is a huge padlock on it and you know that locked inside that chest is all the wisdom you need, all the knowledge you need, all the understanding you need. All the truth you need to grasp is in the box. All the presentation you need is in the box. All the application you need is in the box. Then how do I get at it? You don't get at it by education. You don't get at it by degrees. It has been said that we're "emptying the church by degrees". How do you get at it? The answer is: Christ is the key to all hidden treasures of God's wisdom and knowledge – it is as simple as that. Do you know, the simplest Christian who knows Christ knows more than the greatest philosopher who ever lived? They have found the key. Do you want to grasp truth? Then Christ is the key that unlocks that truth. Do you want to be able to present the truth? Then the best thing you can do is present Christ. Do you want to be able to apply the truth in a given situation? The best thing you can do is to ask Christ about it. He is the key and he is the key to grasping, presenting and applying truth, and that is the mental side of Christianity. If you don't know Christ then you don't have the key.

There are many people in this world who have not got the key to knowledge and understanding and wisdom and it is tragic to see them. They can find out so much about nature. They can find out something about human nature, but if you ask them the deep questions, they haven't a clue. When you ask them why we are here or what their life is for, they look at you and they cannot tell you. They haven't begun to understand. It is one of the facts of life that man in his wisdom cannot find out the truth, that the greatest intellects have been utterly blind when it comes to the truth. I think too of those who have had the key and who have thrown it away, and particularly I think of the nation of Israel.

One's heart burns for Israel because they had the key and they threw it away. All the wisdom and knowledge of God they had locked in their own scriptures and they are still unable to unlock it. They have a treasure chest in their hands. I think of others who have had the key in their hands and unlocked part of the truth and then lost the key. I'm going to mention some of them shortly. So much, then, for Paul's general aim. Since he is speaking about a general aim, the person or pronoun in verses one to three is "they". That "they" may be filled with courage and drawn together in love and have the full wealth of assurance in this way, "they" will know God's secret which is Christ himself—they, they. That is his general aim for all those he has never met and those he has met. For all Christians, that is his general aim—they.

Now he zooms in at Colossae and he changes the pronouns from "they" to "you". He says, "Now I'm very concerned about you." This is the first open hint of trouble at Colossae. He says, "Don't let anyone deceive you with false arguments." The devil will attack you from many quarters. He attacks you morally to take you away from the moral standards of Christ. He attacks you mentally to take you away from the mental stability of knowing Christ. The danger to their faith was that there were people among them with very clever minds and very persuasive arguments, who were leading them away from Jesus Christ. That is an ever-present danger among Christians. I am going to give you three illustrations and three names so that you can understand how it can happen and be on your guard against this danger.

Let me speak first of two men who have helped me personally in my Christian pilgrimage. The first was a famous preacher in London: Dr. Leslie Weatherhead. In my early days when I was feeling after a relationship with God, there was put in my hands a book entitled *The Transforming Friendship*. As a teenager, it gave me the key and I felt I was unlocking treasure. It centred me in on Christ. It was one of the finest modern books about Christ that had been written in the twentieth century. So, having been helped by that book, I bought his other books as they came out. Something began to happen and I began to hear a bit more about Sigmund Freud and Carl Jung and a little less about Jesus Christ. Then came the day when I felt that the insights of Jung and Freud were being used to unlock the secrets of Christ, instead of insights from Christ being used to unlock Jung and Freud. The last great book that he wrote was called *The Christian Agnostic*. The entire book was filled with things about which Dr. Weatherhead was no longer sure. That happened to someone who had helped me.

Let me tell you of another man who helped me enormously. He was my tutor at Cambridge. He took me through Paul's letter to the Romans and he gave me a love for that epistle which has never left me. That man really opened treasures for me in the scriptures and I remember hanging on his words. I still have his notes at home. His name was John Robinson. Later, he left Cambridge and became Bishop of Woolwich. Some rather different things began to come from that man.

Some other names began to come in like Rudolf Bultmann, Paul Tillich and other German philosophers, and John Robinson published the book entitled *Honest to God* and it created a tremendous stir. It was published by the thousand in Japan of all places, where the Shintoists said, "This is just what we believe." That was followed by another book with the title *But that I can't Believe!* Oh, when you read the books they are so persuasive, so reasonable, so logical. They are well put together but something inside one says, "You have lost the key." There isn't treasure here.

Let me now give you a positive example, another man whom I have met and who influenced me positively but after rather than before his crisis. He was the lovely Pakistani Christian Bishop Chandu Ray. As a Hindu he had searched for the truth. His mother had prayed that he would find God and had taken him as a boy to Hindu shrine after Hindu shrine. He never found the truth until one day he found himself at the bedside of a Christian who was going blind and facing a major operation for the removal of his eye, and this Hindu Chandu Ray found himself praying to Jesus for his friend who was a Christian. The Hindu was saying, "Jesus if you're real, heal my friend," and the Lord did. He never had that operation and still, many years later, he can see perfectly. Chandu Ray became a Christian and he was bursting with Christ, and so his church to which he belonged said, "You must go into the ministry." He was sent to an Anglican college in India where he was given theology and philosophy, and given so many insights of other people that he lost the key. He came out of that college having lost the key. He went into the first church where he was to be a priest and a teacher and he got up in the pulpit and preached and he gave them all the stuff he had learned in college. A dear old lady came up to him afterwards and said, "Chandu Ray, you are not preaching Christ." She gave him a little book which was written by a woman living in Reigate in Surrey—Mrs A.M. Hodgkin. Its title was *Christ in all the Scriptures* and it shows that Christ is the key that unlocks Genesis, Exodus, Leviticus, Numbers, Deuteronomy, Joshua, Judges, Ruth, Samuel, Kings, Chronicles, all the way through. Christ unlocks the lot. He said that little old lady brought him back to his faith. He was given back the key. Chandu Ray was later involved in heading up dynamic evangelism in Southeast Asia. Praise God for that little woman who put the key back in his hand.

Many people who go to train for full-time Christian service are so bewildered by so many insights, so many names, so many fashions, that they could lose the key. It is sad when it happens. Do you understand Paul's agony now? Do you understand why he is so anxious that no one with the most reasonable arguments, with a most brilliant intellect should be able to upset someone's faith? He wants them to have the full assurance and to know. He wants them to be able to grasp truth, present truth and apply truth. So don't let anyone persuade you otherwise. How can you tell when these false arguments are coming? Well, I have given you the clue. As soon as a man ceases to use Christ as the key then he is not telling you the truth, however reasonable, however logical, however persuasive his argument may seem—that is the key. That is the key that brings the wealth of God's wisdom into your heart. That is the key you need, and you always will.

So when someone who is quoting a lot of other people, saying, "This is the insight we need" and "That is the insight we need" and "This is the man we need to study" and "That's the man who has at last shown us the truth," don't believe it. Say, "That man is only of value in helping me to understand the truth if he helps me to know Christ better." Praise God, people can help you to know Christ better and Weatherhead,

Robinson and Chandu Ray helped me to know Christ better, but they did so when they were using Christ as the key. That is God's great secret.

Ecclesiastes says, "What can you be sure of?" You can't be sure of men and (I'm afraid he adds) even less sure of women. "You can't be sure of the king. You can't be sure of the future. You can't be sure of public opinion. You can't be sure of justice." What can you be sure of? He finishes up by saying, "The only thing that I can be sure of is that I've enjoyed a good meal today." That is all he can say, and that is all he is sure of. That is why, when I am preaching through Ecclesiastes, I have got to get through to Christ at the end. Because if you stay with Ecclesiastes you stay with human wisdom, and you stay with the most unsatisfactory, unfulfilling, unanswered life. You have to get through and get the key and push the key into the padlock and open it and you can see that all the questions Ecclesiastes asked are answered in Jesus Christ. He is the "Yes and amen" to all God's promises. Do you want to be wise? Do you want to be able to grasp truth? Do you want to be able to apply it in the situations in which you live? Then you need Christ. He is the key to all God's wisdom and knowledge. He is not just a clue, not just a pointer, nor a guideline. He is the key to all God's knowledge and wisdom. No bigger statement could be made about truth than that. It means that the most brilliant scientists, the greatest artists, the most intellectual philosophers, are all in a state of sheer ignorance without this key. It may sound conceited to say it but it is true that the simplest Christian believer has more grasp of truth than the most brilliant sinner.

Let us move on to the last verse of this passage. How are they going to respond to this danger? Are they going to defend the faith or let it go? Are they going to listen to these false teachers and accept the argument? Are they going to drift into their contemporary equivalents of Jung, Freud, Bultmann and Tillich? Are they going to go away from Christ? Are they going to listen to other people or are they going to stay with it?

Here Paul makes a statement, so remarkable that we miss it and therefore misuse it. He says, "I am absent from you in body but I am present with you in spirit." Now if you have ever said that, I wonder if you have meant it. I'm afraid we use the phrase to mean, "I'll be thinking about you," and so somebody who can't turn up to a church meeting says to me, "I've got another engagement but I'll be with you in spirit." What do they mean by that? That they will be thinking about us and praying for us? Well that is fine but it is not being with us in spirit. Paul means something much more than that. Paul is saying that as a Christian I can be in two places at once because his body can be in one place and his spirit can be in another. That can apply to heaven and earth: your body may be on earth and your spirit may take a flight into heaven, whether in the body or out of it you don't know.

But it also applies on earth that a Christian can be in body in one place and in spirit in another. If they are in another place in spirit, they are aware of what is going on in that other place. That is what it is to be present in spirit. So Paul says something quite remarkable here: he has never met them personally, never been to Colossae physically, but he visits them spiritually and can see what's happening. He uses the word "see". Earlier he said, "I heard about you" but now he says, "I see". It is open to the Christian in the Spirit to see things that are happening beyond the reach of his physical eyes. What does he see?

Before we look at that, so that you have got the flavour of what it means to be present in spirit, there was a rather bad situation in Corinth in which a man was sleeping with his stepmother, and Paul wrote to them and said: the man who has done such a thing should be expelled from your fellowship. Even though I am far away from you in body, still I am there with you in spirit. As you meet together and I meet with you in my spirit by the power of our Lord Jesus present with us, you are to hand this man over to Satan for his body to be destroyed.

Did you get the language in this verse? Though Paul is far away from them in body, he is with them in spirit, and as they meet together he meets with them in his spirit, by the power of our Lord Jesus present with us. This is not just, "I'm thinking about you" or "I'm praying for you." This means: "I am present with you. My spirit can see what's happening among you. I'm away here in Rome in prison in my body, but in spirit I am meeting in the church of Colossae. I am watching you, and what do I see?" The picture he sees is thrilling. Do you know what he sees? He uses two military words here. He sees a battlefield – it is a vision in a sense, and he can see the Colossians in the vision. In the vision he sees that they are all closing ranks and getting into line. He uses the word "order", a Greek word (*taxon*) which means soldiers forming into lines. You have seen soldiers do this and get into a line. They will stay there and die if necessary, but no one will shift them because there is nowhere to run, nowhere to retreat – they are a phalanx in closed ranks and they have squared up, facing outwards; the Colossians stand with Christ, and no matter at what point they may be attacked, no matter what argument is used, no matter at what angle others come, trying to persuade them, they will stand solidly in closed ranks and not budge. What a vision!

Paul may be locked up in Rome in prison but he has been to see them in spirit, and he can see it is going to be all right. He can see them closing ranks, forming a square with Christ in the middle, standing close to him and saying, "Nobody's going to shift us." That is so thrilling that Paul rejoices in what he has seen. He is writing to tell them that he has agonised for them, prayed for them. What he saw is what every evangelist, pastor, teacher longs to see, wants to see, and is most thrilled to see: people closing ranks around Jesus and saying, "Nobody, nothing can ever shift us."

In conclusion, a Christian knows more than other people for three reasons. Reason number one: God the Father; reason number two: Jesus Christ; reason number three: the Holy Spirit.

Reason number one, we know more than other people because we can tap God's knowledge and wisdom. There are two ways to truth. One is human discovery, and that way is not open to most of us – we are not clever enough. The other way is divine disclosure and that is the way we found truth. By divine disclosure we have learned more about reality than anybody can learn through human discovery. God has shared his knowledge and wisdom with us.

Reason number two: the Lord Jesus Christ is the key to all the wisdom, and we have the key which no one else has. Reason number three: the Holy Spirit is able to give us extra-sensory perception of reality. A word of wisdom, a word of knowledge – he is able to tell us things that our senses cannot see and cannot find out. So we are not limited as everybody else is to what they see, hear or touch. The Spirit is able to extend our knowledge. So with God the Father's wisdom and knowledge, with Jesus Christ as the key, and being able in the Spirit to find out things that the body cannot find out, do you wonder that Christians are those who know much more than anybody else?

But one final word lest we get too big-headed literally. Christians don't know everything. They need to admit what they don't know. There are times when I have to say, "I don't know what; I don't know when; I don't know why; I don't know how." I have to then add that I do know *who* but it is right for Christians to admit when they don't know. Let me give an illustration of each: I was asked what happens to babies when they die and I had to say, "I don't know, the Bible doesn't say, but I know *who* looks after babies who die and that is all I need."

I don't know when the world is going to end with the winding up of history. I don't know when but I know *who* is going to wind it up. I don't know why some of the finest people in life have to suffer, but I know who does know. I don't know how always to apply the Christian faith to some situations of today which are so complex and not dealt with in God's Word, but I know who can deal with them. So the Christian can say "I know *whom* I have believed," and knowing "whom" is the key to the other questions.

Read Colossians 2:6–23

With the second portion of chapter 2, we are right into the importance of this letter: why it was written, what is concerning Paul that he should write to a church he had never been to and would not know. And he has asked them to send the letter on to another church that he has never been to. The fact is that this book is so rich and so powerful that it can be read by anybody.

The point of this letter is summed up in verse 6 – "So then, just as you received Christ Jesus as Lord, continue to live in him." That is the appeal of the letter – that they should continue in the faith they had when they came to Christ. We have already seen in chapter 1 there is an "if" instead of the introduction – "If you continue in your faith". Then Paul goes on to address the things that will continue with you, if they continue with their faith. So that is the objective of the letter – to get them to *continue* in the faith they once had, and he puts hints of this appeal all the way through, as we shall see.

I have often been corrected in my preaching when I suggested that the word "receive" was never linked with Christ because in modern evangelism, people are being told to *receive Christ* – and that is not a New Testament phrase. I used to say, I don't know of a single text in the New Testament that links the word "receive" with the name "Christ". Everybody came back at me and said: you are wrong; if you look up Colossians 2:6, there it is – "as you received Christ". Now, I am going to defend myself against that charge again because I must give you a little lesson in Greek.

The word translated "received" here is not the normal verb for received. You must take my word for it, or if you know anybody who can do a bit of Greek, check it out with them. The normal Greek word for receive is *lambano*, but here it is not that word, it is *paralambano*, and *para* means "beside". Therefore, this is "just as you received beside". Why should he put that beside – *para* – in front of the word *lambano*, and it becomes *paralambano*? Because that becomes a synonym for the verb "teach". Paul is appealing: stay with what you were taught at the beginning. He knows that they were taught that Jesus is Lord, and he is saying: now stay there – do not let anybody take you off course; do not let anybody with deceptive philosophy distract you from this statement. You learned the simplicity of Christ and you became and, as we have seen, "Christ" is one of the new titles given to Jesus when Peter preached at Pentecost. He finished his sermon with this vital word – this Jesus whom you crucified, God has made him Lord and *Christ*. That is the full Christian faith and if anybody says "our Lord Jesus Christ" you can be sure that he or she is fully in the Christian faith. We shall see that combination of Lord and Christ come up again and again.

So then, just as you were taught, Christ Jesus is Lord, remain in him, rooted and grounded, continue to live in him. Do not let anything distract you from Christ. That is a very passionate appeal in his heart, because if you can sever and separate from Christ someone who had belonged to him, then you have achieved a mighty distraction. By the way, there can be someone in a person's background who taught them the full truths of the gospel. There were two men that I admired tremendously. They were Red Skelton and Branse

Burbridge and they were my heroes at the time I became a Christian because they both believed in our "Lord Jesus Christ" (all three words). They were both spitfire pilots and they were both honoured by the King George VI with the Distinguished Flying Cross. I met them and thought: I would love to be like those two. And they were introduced to me as full Christians who had been among "the few" to whom we owed so much in 1942. It was shortly after that I became a member of the RAF.

The big question to me was how two pilots who had saved Britain during the war use the term "our Lord Jesus Christ"? I remember wrestling with that question for some time and then I gave in, and I called the Lord Jesus Christ, full names and titles, and became a Christian. I have never since looked back. I knew if I did look back I would lose everything worthwhile, because the fullness of God dwells in his Son bodily.

Charles Wesley ended one verse of one of his six thousand hymns with the phrase "incomprehensibly made man", and he was praising the godhead who became compressed into a man. That is a primary thing to believe. It might seem impossible to believe that he would do such a thing, but God did it and knew what he was doing. That is called the Incarnation, which means *in flesh*.

The people at Colossae were in danger of losing Christ and therefore losing their fullness in Christ because, as he said, every bit of knowledge was squeezed into that one man. So why go to anybody else, when you have got contact direct with the one man who squeezed all of God into his person? You cannot afford to lose him because you would lose your own fullness. Christ is your fullness and the fullness of God is so real in him that he is all you need – and oh, what a horror that other men should separate us from Christ, which is what some men were doing in Colossae. In the rest of chapter 2 you get the hint of these men and what they were teaching, and what they were like and where they had come from.

What were they teaching? First of all, they were teaching religious festivals. They were teaching them on a three-fold basis: festivals that came once a year, festivals that came once a month and festivals that came weekly, and he said that you should have nothing to do with any of them. I suppose the hardest for Christians to have nothing to do with is the Sunday which is believed by so many to fulfil the Sabbath of the Old Testament. There is not a line in the New Testament that ties Sunday to the Sabbath but I know many Christians have done just that. And that is one little step away from Christ, for Christ himself claimed to be the Lord of the Sabbath, and that means he is the boss for your Sabbath. You do things on the Sabbath because of him, but actually if you make Sunday a Sabbath, you have fallen into their trap because Jesus said that he is the Lord of the Sabbath which means that you ask him about anything you are called to do on Sunday – and Monday and Tuesday and Wednesday and Thursday and Friday and Saturday. None of those is a Sabbath to the Christian. They are all the Lord's days to the Christian and therefore he is the Lord of your Sabbath. That was one thing they were teaching. Along with it, they taught dietary laws. Food and drink are such a large part of everybody's life and pleasure.

I have been in trouble for being anti-Sabbath, but I believe that Sabbath was the shadow. Jesus Christ is the reality. But once you have the reality, you do not have the shadows.

That brought to my mind a fairy story I loved as a child. In it, a girl became an orphan and was packed away into an orphanage and there the man who had provided the orphanage visited it regularly and she saw his shadow, but not in reality. She saw the shadow of this visitor on the wall of the corridor and she called him "Daddy Longlegs" after the insect. The book finishes superbly. In the story they met at last when she was grown up and she really fell in love with what she had worshipped as a shadow all her life, and he was no longer "Daddy Longlegs" but he was the real thing! She was now Mrs Real Thing. It is a lovely story, a real romance, and so well written, you are with it, and you are into the wedding at the end.

Surely the church could not be distracted from Christ with celebrations daily, weekly, monthly (called "new moon Sabbaths") and annually, could they? Would the church ever fall for such a thing? The answer, horrifically, is Christmas. I am afraid I am going to destroy all your romanticism about Christmas, not because I like destroying things, but because it is the biggest delusion that has captured the whole church and I have, all my ministry, told people that I am not a Christmas man. Yet, it produces tremendous pressure on me. Every bit of Christmas that we celebrate has a pagan origin. Carols have a pagan origin, and frankly, they do not tell the story correctly anyway. It was not in a "bleak mid-winter" and Jesus, as a baby did cry! It is the only way a baby can tell its parents that he is hungry and needs food.

When did Christians first celebrate Christmas? I will tell you, and this is the truth. Pope Gregory was a well-known Pope in Roman Catholic history and he sent missionaries to England and they came in by a small river in Kent to the place that is now called Canterbury. The first missionary was called Augustine and he settled there and so, after a year or two, Pope Gregory said: send in a report as to how effectively you are getting on. I need to know if we have sent you and wasted you. So Augustine sent him a daily report because, he said: We are doing fine. Kings are being baptised and we are really making headway. But, he said, there is a downside – we can't get them to stop celebrating their midwinter festival in which they not only celebrate the midwinter, but bring in gods of another kind including Mithras the god of the sun. And he was at the celebrations because the sun was renewed twelve days earlier. When they were sure the sun had come back for another year, they threw themselves into this Yule celebration. I am sure you have heard of the yule log because there was always a big bonfire at the heart of the festival. Again, they made it a matter of diet – they all over-ate and over-drank at the festival. Is there anything new in plum pudding or turkey? No, it is all pagan. They said that this festival had such a hold on people that they could not be persuaded to drop it when they became Christians. So they asked Pope Gregory: what shall we do about that? It is failure if you cannot get them off their pagan culture. And he said a very important thing. If he had known the phrase, he would have said: if you can't lick them, join them. I am afraid that became the official policy of Roman Catholic evangelism – baptise the culture into Christ, and therefore, they will all come to celebrate Christ and we will have a special mass for them – Christ-mass – which is where they got the word "Christmas". And that has become a devastating evangelistic motto.

When I went to South America, I was astonished that converts to Christ were celebrating the dead and communicating with them, which we know as spiritualism. I asked why Catholics were practising spiritualism. They told me that it was this missionary policy of baptising the culture into Christ and the result is also that when you go to the Philippines you will be shocked at how many people are playing with spirits – as if they had a spiritualist missionary. It is the same in every country where they have had Roman Catholic missionaries – they baptise the culture into Christ by calling it Christ-mas.

People have noticed that I do not get excited about Christmas and have asked me what I think about it. I reply that I do not think anything about it; I don't believe in it. Then they say: You don't believe in Christmas? Weren't you a minister of the gospel? You don't believe in Christmas; why don't you? And I have replied: because I am a Christian. You would really be amazed at the response that has brought. To me there is no contradiction. If you go through the things that the church does or has, you will find that they did not stop at Christmas. They went way beyond that. Have you heard the saying "touch wood"? That means touching a crucifix for "luck".

Quite early in my ministry, I tried to wean people off Christmas. I was called Ebenezer Scrooge, and I don't know what else. It was colossal pressure, and it costs you, believe me. You are a social misfit again, and that is only too well directed at you.

Do you walk under ladders? Why not? You see, things become human traditions and the ways of the world have crept into the church in an alarming way. Jesus never told us to celebrate Christmas. He told us to celebrate his death, not his birth, and we celebrate his death whenever we have Communion – which can be every Sunday, but we don't observe it just *because* it is weekly.

We see what was happening to the church at Colossae. They had numerous false teachers coming in, who claimed to be Christians, and they had enough of the Christian gospel in them to fool people, yet out of it was coming a church that judged you by whether you accepted their traditions.

I do not mind a midwinter festival, especially when they say it is for kids, but I would never tell them we owe this to Jesus. He was not born on December 25th, but there is just a possibility that he was conceived on December 25th because he was born nine months after that, at the time of the Feast of Tabernacles. That is when I celebrate the coming of Jesus.

The false teachers were bringing in some rather peculiar notions of worship, and it was an entirely new style of worship for the Christians. They also held a mock humility, an artificial humility, and it shone through them whenever they talked. They did not push themselves, they were not arrogant, but they taught with a pseudo authority that convinced many of the people to whom Paul was writing.

Now that is one aspect of this false teaching and there it is in 2:16, but once you have been warned about these things, expect false teachers to try to rob you of Christ. Because when you have other teachers you are taught other things and your attention is switched from Christ.

I will acknowledge one thing before we leave this. Many years ago, I was invited to be a chairman of a Commission of the Evangelical Alliance, which is the biggest union of evangelicals in this country. I met the commission as a body, and they were prominent Christians. It was a select and elitist body made of some of the best evangelicals in this country. As chairman of the commission, I said that the first meeting we have must be of prayer to get us right with God before we start telling other people what they should be doing. They gathered for prayer and someone (I don't know who) suggested that we ask Jesus himself what there was in his church that he could not cope with. Now it sounds a funny thing for a prayer request, but we all knelt down and we prayed quite a bit, and then we asked Jesus what there was in the church that he deplored. Like lightning, to three separate people, there came the word "Christmas". I have not enjoyed Christmas ever since that night. Very few people are prepared to ask Jesus, the Lord of the Sabbath, about Christmas, and therefore Christ does not get a good look in. Now it is so commercialised that it begins in August. Christmas cards are signed and so on. I just cannot join in. It worries me and it actually makes it painful when I see people eating and drinking too much and doing it all in the name of Jesus.

But there is another list of things that they taught: a list of rules and regulations. Three rules are mentioned: do not handle, do not taste, do not touch. Versions of those have again found their way into our faith. What you could say is that all this chapter is written to stop Christianity becoming a religion. Because when you say that Christianity is Christ and you really live with that, and Christ is really Lord of your life, that in itself is a testimony. But you will find other things like "touching wood" that have come into Christian living, diverting attention from the Lord Jesus Christ. So if you live for Christ you are out of line with the popular norm. As soon as you make it known what you stand for in Christ, you find you are on the losing side.

You are also in the Christianity that is Christ and I want to suggest that you also ask him about some of the things you are doing. I hope that they are troubling you in the sense that you do not feel comfortable with them. Our objection is not just the commercialisation, but that people do not really know who was born. Fewer people come to Christ at Christmas than at any other time of the year. There are fewer and fewer evangelistic crusades if any at that time. You will find some at Easter because that becomes a little more Christian but quite frankly, I am trying to get Christ out of Christmas because it is an insult to him. I discovered how he feels about it, and that he hates being worshipped as a little baby and not worshipped as a man and as God in whom the whole godhead dwelt bodily. Paul sets out the areas in which the false teachers were gaining ground: the areas of festival – annual, monthly and weekly celebrations of the Christian faith.

The one snag with adopting the Christianising of culture is that you cannot help pulling in with that the pagan culture from which it comes. I don't think you can stop Christmas – it has too big a hold on everybody in church as well as everybody outside church, and I am very disturbed at the impressive support for it.

There are two areas of the world's religions that we have adopted: these regular celebrations and the fact of being too negative. The ways of the world are very interesting. This world is full of religion and there are in every atlas maps of the religions. Have you seen those? I have a global map of where my ministry is going at the moment and it is very encouraging. It is getting a foothold in Russia – and in countries where paganism is mostly the ruler of the day.

This would not be a Christian epistle unless there were inserted the answer, showing why we are in a position to deal with the matter. In 2:6, Paul's first appeal is to go on, rooted and grounded in Christ, and to let all their growth and attention be in Christ, and in all that they want to do to refer to Christ first. So there it is: Continue to live in him, rooted and built up in him, strengthened in the faith as you were taught, overflowing with thankfulness. For the rest of the epistle, the word "thankfulness" keeps coming in. The Christian life is a life of gratitude, and even if you are thinking as I have been outlining, you can be thankful that you know the truth. So: be thankful, be thankful, be thankful. The Greek for "I thank you" is *eucharisto* and the church has even pulled that in and attached it to the Mass or Communion. We are not a negative religion – don't do this, don't do that, don't do the other.

A negative religion is again a worldly religion. These regulations come in from the wrong source. I cannot help thinking of Martin Luther before he was a Christian. He would whip himself with a real whip until he collapsed on the floor of his monastic cell out of sheer exhaustion. Then one day he found the truth as he gave a lecture on Romans and his superior in the hierarchy, who was in charge of his spiritual growth, said: Martin, you've cut out true religion, you've cut out Mass, you've cut out saints' days. You're wrecking all the aids to devotion and robbing Christians of all the things that they trust in. What will you put in their place? Luther gave his historic answer: Christ. The people only need Christ. That has become the fixed memory of the Reformation. They don't need all these things.

Ah, but some say, they do need them to have help with their devotion to Christ. His answer: that all they need is Christ! That was the heart of Martin Luther's Reformation. You might let your faith depend on something else; I remember going to Knock, a big Roman Catholic pilgrimage centre because an image of the Virgin Mary appeared on the end wall of the church. They have built a magnificent, huge shrine, to which hundreds of Catholics are thronging, and I dropped in to see that. I was curious, and the pressure to join in was colossal. There was a row of petty shops along the high street selling rubbish, trinkets of all kinds. They persuade you to buy something from Knock to take with you and use in your devotions, such as the obvious crucifixes. Christ was just not there. Everything else was there. Hundreds of thousands of people are flying into Knock where they have built an airport to cope. Christ never intended that.

There are still other things that we have brought in from paganism, and I will mention another – splitting the Body of Christ into amateurs and professionals: clergy and laity. That has infected every church and we cannot avoid the pressure.

So that is the first appeal: continue to live in him, ruled and built up in him. Then see to it that no-one takes you captive through hollow and deceptive philosophy which depends on human tradition and the basic principles of this world rather than on Christ. We now turn to 2:9, "For in Christ all the fullness of the deity dwells in bodily form and you have been given fullness in Christ who is head over every power and authority." That is a tremendous privilege. There is nothing in God that you do not find in Jesus and if you have accepted Christ, you have accepted the fullness of God and now there is nothing new you can desire outside of Christ.

Now then comes a very difficult passage. Peter in his letter says there are many difficult things in Paul's letters – and this is one of them. Paul says you were all circumcised. There is a real study needed on the relation of Paul to circumcision. He was circumcised himself and he circumcised Timothy but fought against circumcision all his life. He was against circumcision. It comes up in letter after letter – the letter to the Galatians, for example. If Paul was against something, it was circumcision. And that was due to Jews who followed him around in his missionary journeys and as soon as he got some converts, there came the Jews to circumcise them, teaching them you cannot be a full Christian without circumcision because you become a Jew first and then you are required to follow the Jews in the Messiah Jesus the Christ. So Paul had to fight against circumcision and here he is saying that everybody is circumcised in Christ. Do you get that tension? We have got to unravel the unusual teaching now of Paul, that you were also circumcised. That means everybody who was converted under Paul, men and women, were told they were circumcised. Why? It is one of the deep teachings of Paul; his theory is, whatever Christ has gone through, I have gone through with him. And that is Christian attitude to culture.

If you find that difficult, Christ died on a cross – so did you. Christ was raised from the tomb – so were you. We accept God did it, but here he is saying: Christ was circumcised, so are you. What does he mean? This is one of the difficult things that Paul taught that we must unravel until we can teach and believe in it. His theory was this: Christ on the cross died to everything connected with his nature as a man. He died to everything connected with the flesh, and "flesh" for him was not a nice word. It means all that you were in your birth, and he said you were cut off from all that because you are a Christian. But I'll tell you what the real thing is. Circumcision is to have a little bit of your flesh cut off, and particularly the male flesh. To the Jew, his circumcision was the symbol of his faith; it was what reminded him every day that he was of God's people. Pride came in and a Jew is very proud of his circumcision. It is a mark no-one can remove.

Jesus was circumcised on the eighth day of his life. It made him a Jew and he became a devout Jew. He took all their "don'ts" and he absorbed Judaism into his flesh and then died on the cross where naturally all his flesh became dead. That is what circumcision is. For the Jew it was a cutting off of part of his flesh. For the Christian, he is circumcised with the circumcision of Christ. But it is the circumcision that Jesus experienced on the cross when he was literally cut off from all flesh, and so Paul is interpreting the cross here and telling us that one meaning of the cross is that Jesus had all his flesh cut off, all his past cut off, everything that belonged to him by birth cut off. He makes his point very powerfully – and that is exactly what has happened to the Christian. You have said goodbye to your old life; you have completely cut it off, and you should not be showing it again. This epistle is making "therefore" the key word in Christian literature, and he is constantly saying you have died with Christ, you have been raised with Christ, you have been circumcised with Christ. That is a truth that we need to know, but you never hear sermons on it, partly because there are now women present in every congregation and it is considered indiscreet. This is his sole thrust and will be in the next chapter particularly: For this you have died in Christ; you have been raised with Christ. When? The answer is very simple: when you were baptised. That is when you cut yourself off from your past, and Christ was coming in to take the place of all your past.

You can approach it through the death of Christ. I can remember my baptism – funnily enough, it was years after I became a Methodist minister. I was baptised (but don't tell anyone) about thirteen years after I became a Christian. I was crucified with Christ and now my calling is to work that out in my life. All is forgiven, yet the secret is that you have already had crucifixion but now you must put to death everything associated with the past. That makes Christian living a matter of putting to death all that belonged to your old self. That is really the next chapter, but we are bound to ask what it says to people: you need to start with this – that you have been crucified with Christ; you have been buried with Christ; you have been raised with Christ – and "raised" there does not include just the resurrection, though it includes that, but also the ascension. You have been raised. A Christian's home address is heaven. That already is your address but you have not really worked it all out. Putting to death things that were you can be very painful, it can be a drawn out problem, but it is the answer to all non-regular observance, not regulations that say "Don't do this".

So Christianity starts with a repetition of *Christ in you*. So that has already happened; it is already accomplished. It does not need to be done again. What is needed is to work out the implications of that. God has worked it in, now you work it out. That is how it all happens.

Now I am touching here on something that is quite deep. *Your identification with Christ is the important thing*. That is your starting point and God has worked that into your life, but now you need to work it out. Blessed are those who will work it out and really mean business in cutting off all the flesh that brought in these things. We begin to realise that the people have lived pretty dirty lives before. They were not nice people. So if Paul is here trying to stop Christianity becoming a religion (and that means to the loss of Christ), then that is the heart of his letter.

When I taught on this passage, I was asked a question: We are dead in Christ, but the old man seems to linger. So, what can we do about this old man that doesn't seem to want to die but keeps coming back? My reply was that I know it sounds drastic, but we have to kill the "old man"! We have been crucified; now crucify the old self. That is the heart of what Paul is saying and it is painful. You have to crucify all that you were, and that is not easy.

So is "killing" this "old man" just an act of will? In a sense it is comforting that Paul acknowledges there *is* an "old man" still around. All of us are conscious sometimes under extreme pressure that other people (maybe the church) may be pulling you toward something. You feel the pressure of other people. That is what needs to be cut, and it may cost you friendship.

I am going to give you two simple illustrations that might help you to understand and to apply the truth. The first is of a man whom I went to see in hospital. His leg was very bad, it had gone gangrenous and he was in great pain. They were trying to kill the pain with drugs, but they were unable to do so. He really was in agony with this leg. I remember him saying to me, "Oh, Pastor, I just want them to take the leg off. I don't mind losing it, just take it off," and finally they did.

I went to see him about two or three days later. His face looked perplexed and he was troubled. He was suffering from what is called "Phantom Limb". He said, "I thought when they took my leg off they would take away the feelings of it, but you know, the feelings haven't gone away. I can feel my toes, I can feel my leg, but I now cannot scratch. I cannot touch them." It is a well-known medical fact that, on losing the limb, the central nervous system, having been tuned for so long to having a limb there, goes on feeling it and therefore the problem of feelings remains.

Now, I want to say that in exactly the same way, even though I have been crucified with Christ, and have shared his circumcision and had the flesh cut away, the central nervous system has been so tuned to that old man that the feelings are still there. That is what Paul is going to teach later in the letter. Feelings of lust, feelings of greed, feelings of anger, feelings of pride – in chapter three he is going to deal with these. He is going to teach Christians that you have to deaden these feelings – you must put them to death. They are real feelings, but they do not correspond to real facts. A process of re-education is going to have to go on. So my brother whom I was visiting in hospital had to learn to adjust his thinking and re-educate his mind to accept that his leg was not there, even though all his feelings told him it was, and that he must adjust to that and think that way, then he could accept and integrate. In the same way, Paul is teaching: you have died with Christ, therefore put to death the feelings that belonged to what has been cut away.

Do you get the message now? It means that the secret of living the Christian life is to gear your feelings to the *facts*. Let us get a clear grasp of what actually has happened – that the old life has gone. Let us get those things that still remind us of that old life killed. It is as if you lived with someone and they died, but you kept all their clothes in the wardrobe, you kept all their little things around so that their very presence still seemed real. It seemed as if they just got away temporarily. It is as if Paul is saying: go around the house, get those clothes out of that wardrobe and get rid of them; get rid of everything that reminds you of that life that died and was buried; get rid of it all. Indeed later, in chapter three, he puts it in terms of clothes: put off the clothes that the old man used to wear; do not go on wearing those things, put on the things that the new man is going to wear.

So if you died with Christ, then put these things to death. If you have risen with Christ, then seek the things that are above. In other words, become what you already are.

To try to get that truth home a little further, let me give you another illustration. When we were living in Buckinghamshire the local newspaper said that a jobbing gardener in Buckinghamshire had inherited both a title and a fortune. This man, who trundled his wheelbarrow and tools around every day, was now "Lord" somebody, with a fabulous fortune. But he chose to go on being a jobbing gardener and he went on trundling his wheelbarrow and tools. It was true that he was a lord, and it was true that he was wealthy, but he did not feel like it because he did not appropriate it at first.

Paul's teaching means: enter into your position; claim your title. This has already happened. You have shared in the death, in the burial, in the resurrection of Jesus, then why are you not enjoying it? Why are you not living his risen life – or rather, letting him live it in you – since you have buried that old life? So the rest of this letter you will find is simply this: possess your possessions; claim your title, realise the facts. Even though your feelings are all against these facts, claim the facts. Let your faith rest on the facts, not your feelings.

I know you have feelings of struggle. I know you have feelings that the "old man" is still around. I know you have this tension that Romans chapter 7 describes so clearly: the good I would, I do not, and the evil that I would not, that I do. I know that Paul was writing there as a Christian when he wrote: with my mind I accept the law of God. With my mind I believe all this. But somehow my members keep behaving in a different kind of way. There is a real tug here.

Well, the answer to this conflict, the answer to this tension is to let your faith go towards the facts rather than the feelings, and say: the fact is I am crucified, I am buried, I am raised; therefore, Lord, I am in a position to remove the clothes of the old man, to remove the habits, to remove the pressures.

But you will never do it by yourself. The secret lies in Romans chapter 8. It is the law of the Spirit of life who sets you free from the law of death. It is the law of the Spirit of life that enables the fact to change your feelings and to give the victory.

You can prove this. If you think what I have been giving you here is a lot of theoretical theology, then I challenge you to prove it as I did. I was awake fairly early one day, and as I was just lying there I remembered a verse I had read the previous night: "I lie awake in the night thinking of you." So it was appropriate that that word was given to me the night before. But I did not think of it immediately. Something from my old nature came first in the hours of semi-waking, a time when you are not at your best and not alert.

My mind went back to a little Baptist chapel in the Pennine hills, and a rather green, slimy baptistry pool that had not been used in years. I declared to the enemy: "I was buried there and I was raised there, so get away." It took less than one minute for him to go. My feelings could have run away with me, but the facts held me. Then I lay awake and thought of the Lord.

Now do you understand the practicality of this? Claim it, believe it, and apply it, for it is true. We are not trying to brainwash ourselves; we are not trying to delude ourselves. In fact, it is the phantom self that is deluding us. It is the feelings that have been left behind that are deluding us. We call Satan's bluff and we go right back to the beginning of our Christian life and say: "I died, I was buried, I was raised, I believed in a God who could do this to my flesh. So just you get away from me."

Read Colossians 3:1–17

Now this is the heart of Paul's letter to the Colossians; these 17 verses contain the essence of what he wanted to say to them: *You are this, so therefore do that.* It is a very powerful argument to Christians and it puzzles us because he is addressing all the Christians at Colossae and he says this has happened to you: you have all died with Christ; you have all been raised with Christ; you have all been circumcised in Christ. It is an extraordinary claim for Christians, and an extraordinary argument of the obligations a Christian has because of what has happened to him or her.

Other people can try to be as good, but they have not got that start. They cannot say, "I've been crucified with Christ; I am dead with Christ; I have been raised with Christ." But we who are believers can say that. It makes a huge difference to the way we live. Or it is bound to if we really work through it. We saw in chapter 2 the appeal of this letter: just as we received Christ Jesus as Lord, continue to live in him, rooted and built up in him, strengthened in the faith as you were taught, overflowing with thankfulness.

I want to ask an important question which I will not answer immediately, namely: when did all this happen to you? Because Paul presents all these things as fact. You have been crucified with Christ. You are alive in Christ. It has all happened to you. But when did it happen to us? I will try to answer that question later.

I could title this chapter "Secret of a Saint" because this is the real secret behind Christians who live right, and if they have done it right, then they have made it. We have no doubt as to what Paul's objective is: he wants to present you *perfect*! That word comes frequently in these chapters. It is a terrific ambition, to want to present people perfect. The world will simply say: no-one's perfect, so why even try? But I am trying because that is my ambition too – to present everyone perfect. That is our goal, perfection, which is quite an extraordinary goal. I keep telling my wife that one day I will be perfect, and she finds it so hard to believe, but there it is. I tell her that I have got to believe that one day she will be perfect, and that is a bit easier for me to believe than her to believe about me, but there we are. That is the goal of a Christian: perfection. We aim to be perfect people and that is a huge ambition. This chapter tells us the secret behind becoming perfect. The secret is to realise what you already are, because what you already are was God's work in you, and he put those things together in you so that he might make you perfect, and that is a great ambition of God which he has shared with Paul.

So let us begin with the first few verses here which present the kind of argument of the "since then" people, or the "therefore" people. Because of this, therefore do that… is the argument and it is irresistible. Chapter 3 begins, Since then you have been raised with Christ. He has been raised, and so have we, and "raised" includes the ascension, which means frankly that every real Christian is already in heaven. They don't go to heaven when they die; they just wake up in heaven where they have been in theory for so long. Since then you have been raised with Christ, set your hearts on things above and set your minds on things above. There we have a person whose thoughts and feelings are often in heaven and that is a funny place to be, but that is our address really. I remember a pastor telling me that in Germany he was in the German Youth there, which was where all young German people had to be, and when they joined the German Youth, they were asked this question: Where do you live? What's your address? This pastor as a young man had said, "I live in Germany."

"Wrong answer; where do you live?"

Then he said, "In the Third Reich" – or the third kingdom, which is what Hitler called Germany.

"Wrong answer; where do you live?"

He replied, "I'm sorry, I can't think of the right answer. What is the right answer?"

His questioner said, "The right answer is – Hitler – I live in Hitler. That's my address."

That was what they taught all the youth in Germany in the Hitler Youth to say, and they taught them to live that way and constantly to be thinking of Hitler, the leader of the Third Reich, the ruler of Germany, and that they should be constantly turning their hearts to him, and constantly turning their minds to him – so that he gradually filled all their life.

That man had grown up and become a Christian and changed his life, and if you ask him now, "Where is your address; where do you live?" he simply says, "I live in Christ – that's my new address." That is very real to him. He is not embarrassed to say, "I live in Christ." That is what these first few verses are about: that where Christ is you should set your mind, and set your heart – which is out of this world. That will help you to live a heavenly life on earth and be a saint.

Actually Christ calls every Christian a saint, but I am afraid not all of them are saints, as we find out only too quickly. This is written – how to be a saint in church – and that is why it says forgive each other as Christ forgave you. The best context to live a saintly life is the church, with all its faults and with all its imperfect people. That is the ideal place for you to learn to be a saint, and that is probably a new thought to you.

Then Paul goes on to explain why your real life is hidden in Christ. He is your *real* life. He is your address. But that is not visible to anybody on earth. They may ask questions – good. But they don't know where you really live. The answer is: you really live in heaven. That is where your life is hidden – with Christ in God. One day, Christ will appear in glory to everybody on earth and therefore, with him, you will also have a revealed life and everybody will know where you have really been living – in Christ, in heaven. Your mind and heart are set on that address, and that is bound to come out in your life if it is properly believed. That is when your life appears. It appears when his life appears. You are already in heaven so it will not be a strange place to you when you die. It is just like going to sleep and waking up in another place in which you already were. Your body has ceased to say, "I'm in Basingstoke" or wherever, because your senses tell you that you live on earth and your senses tell you that you are really living down here. It is a constant battle for a Christian to remind himself or herself that their life is in heaven.

That is the first three verses. We leave them because the next verse says "put to death". A Christian who is seeking above and looking up for their focal point realises there are things they have got to put to death. Being a saint of God is putting to death, and what they put to death makes them saints. Put to death, therefore.... One of the "therefores" that is very important to a Christian is that they have put to death certain things. And here Paul is saying: put to death therefore everything that belongs to your own life. That is a very practical thing.

For some, it may be the television set; for others, places it may be where they used to go. It is good when Christians do put these things to death. Paul lists some of those things: immorality, impurity, lust (those things are all related); evil desires and greed. Many Christians would say that greed is just a natural weakness, that you are made that way. No! That is one of the bits of the old life you have to murder – and sometimes murder is very costly. I have known people in Christ who have put things to death and who have found it one of the hardest things to do because it was one of the habitual things in their previous life. Paul is saying: you used to walk in these ways. You used to live right here.

I remember preaching once to a new church in a new building in Milton Keynes and, towards the end of my sermon, a young lad got up and he ran out of the church and a quarter of an hour later, he came back in carrying all his heavy rock music discs. He came to the front of the audience, and he took them up one by one and cracked them. That was his response and it was so real to him. You could see it was costing him to rip up those records, but they were part of his old life which was leading him astray and he lived in them and he was just obeying this verse.

I remember we once had a pipe and a tobacco pouch in the bottom of the baptistry in the church at Millmead and I understood that perfectly well. The man we were "burying in water" was putting to death something that had been part of his life for a long time and it was his comfort. I have often thought that people with pipes in their mouths looked a bit like babies with dummies. But put to death therefore everything that belonged to your old life. Sometimes your heart is being torn if it has been too attached to something. It is costly to put the dagger in and murder it. Paul is being quite honest here: you used to live like this.

There is one bit of information about Colossae which we did not have. It was on the main road between Europe and Asia and therefore it was full of inns and bars and all the paraphernalia of a town that is on the main route. We don't think of that much. We think of Colossae as a town that had a very good church in it. But that was the background of the church. The members had been like that. So Paul is under no illusions about the church. From here to the rest of these verses he is using as a picture of the Christian life a person who chooses what he wears – *clothes* himself. He puts on certain clothes and he puts off certain clothes. In fact, they are in the perfect tense which means they have already put these things off and put on new clothes. He lists the things that they are now putting off and says that you must murder them because you have put them off. You have stopped wearing them. You have put on... then he lists a whole new lot of things that they have put on.

It sounds so easy to say that all you have got to do is put things off and put things on. Isn't that easy? No, it is very hard. It means that, as you dress in the morning, you choose what you are going to wear for the day and you choose Christ to wear. It goes on: clothe yourselves as God's chosen people, holy and dearly loved. Clothe yourselves with compassion, kindness, humility, gentleness and patience. Aren't those lovely clothes to wear? You can put them on in the morning by a conscious alignment to Christ. Christ, this is what you were; this is what you are, and therefore, this is what I am. There is this putting off the rags of your previous life and putting on the new clothes of Christ instead.

Then comes some very realistic talk about being in a company of people where you are going to have to bear one another, and I am afraid that is true also. The Lord has a funny people, a funny family. In my previous church but one, the one back in Buckinghamshire, there was a dear old lady and she really was Christlike. But she said so many times to me after a service: The Lord has a funny family, David. I used to say to her: yes and you are in it and I am in it, and we are part of that funniness that has made it difficult for other people to live with it. If you find people in your church difficult to live with, it is an ideal context to develop this, the ideal background to put on the right clothes. When did they put off all their old clothes? When did they put on these new clothes? When did it happen? The same question that I want to come back to.

Now, as God's chosen people, holy and dearly loved, bear with one another and forgive whatever grievance you may have against one another – it sounds almost as if we should expect to have grievances against one another. It can happen in church life – I can guarantee that. However well you have chosen the church you go to, you will still find it difficult; there will still be people who don't fit in with you and those are the people you are to love. So Paul says: above all these virtues, put on love which binds them all together. That is the ultimate "putting on". If you have learned the art of getting up in the morning and putting on – clothing yourself – with love, you have mastered being a saint and that is the secret. You find yourself letting the peace of Christ rule your heart – and that is quite an achievement. In fact, he says "let the peace of Christ" three times. Let the peace of Christ be an important part of your daily "putting on".

You do that as a member of one Body and you did not choose the other members. Even in the best fellowship you know, there are people with whom you would not choose to be in fellowship. It is just the way it works out. That is when you let the peace of Christ come in. These things are characteristic of saints: the peace of Christ; gratitude – thankfulness. That also is mentioned three times here so here we are building up a picture. You and I have known saints who were peaceful people and brought peace with them when they came, and you find yourself longing to be like that. They are thankful people – always grateful. With the peace and the gratitude, you have two of the most wonderful things that you can have as a member of the Body.

Let the word of Christ dwell in you richly as you teach and admonish one another with all wisdom. There is a rare thing to see in a Christian fellowship – admonition, correcting one another, but doing it in love. If you try correcting without love, you are in trouble; but with love it is a sheer privilege to be correcting one another. At this point Paul brings in an unusual note: "While you are singing to one another...." And he mentions three kinds of song – the ordinary kind of song to one another, hymns which have specially been written for Christians to sing, and spiritual songs where both the words and music are being given by the Spirit to someone, and they are singing to you, admonishing you because it is of the Holy Spirit and it is done in love. Here is a mention of what they did when they came together as a community – they sang three kinds of songs. I have heard all three kinds, and spiritual songs are beautiful. I don't know if you have heard spiritual songs where the Holy Spirit is giving the music, the tune, and the lyrics – the words – are lovely. But they go right to your heart and seem to have a spearhead on them. What a joy they are to hear.

From that, Paul launches into a very simple theme: whatever you do in word or deed – *whatever* covers everything – do it all in the name of the Lord Jesus. That is sainthood; that is what we are after.

Well now, let's tackle the big question. When were the basic things happening? Because they are what God is doing himself towards your sainthood. God will do those basic things: your death with Christ, your resurrection with Christ and your circumcision with Christ. I found that amazing in chapter 2 – this circumcision with Christ. Paul was known all his life for being anti-circumcision and in many of his letters, he denounces Christians for wanting to be circumcised. He did circumcise one of his team, Timothy, so that he could actually enter Jewish homes and evangelise them. But he did not do this as a regular thing. He was against circumcision. He then talks about Christ being circumcised on the cross which meant he was cutting off all of his past human life, and then Paul says that is what should happen to you – cutting out of your life all that does not please God, and therein reveals the motivation of the saint. In theory, he is now a person who does everything to please God, and therefore he knows when he is doing something that does not please God.

Then comes this hard statement: Because of all these things in your past life, the wrath of God is coming. Saints are to fear the wrath of God and I get this quite plainly from this passage and many others – that saints can drift into a life that is no longer pleasing God, and therefore it is storing up the wrath of God for themselves. The wrath of God is very real in the New Testament, both before you are a Christian and, here, after you are a Christian, and it is something to be feared – the anger of God. It is widespread and it can be seen in our society.

I heard recently of a man who is noted for hearing God and issuing prophecies for us to take note of, and he gave a very profound prophecy recently. The first thing in it was: Brexit is his will for Britain. This prophet said: God says, we must come out of Europe. I had been thinking that way for a long time and speaking that way a bit, but that is a profound thing in our current society. It is right and proper that we come out of Europe and do not go down the sink with her. The second part of the prophecy was that Europe is living in a way that is going to draw the wrath of God on it. That is something worth knowing.

When did all this happen to me as a Christian? When did I die with Christ? When was I raised with Christ? When was I circumcised with Christ? That is a crucial question raised by this passage. The answer is this, as far as I can make it out: in your baptism as a believer! That is when it happened. In fact, in that "circumcised with Christ" passage in chapter 2, it specifically mentions your baptism and it is assuming your baptism is the baptism of a believer in Christ Jesus.

I have made an awful lot of baptism in my life and that has had a profound effect on a lot of people, but I take baptism very seriously not for what it looks like but for what God does in baptism. God does something in that act that you can get nowhere else, and I believe this is what Paul is hinting at all the way through here. Your baptism into Christ was a supreme act of obedience to Christ. It is then that you were baptised into Christ, and it is then that the substitution took place, and God treated you as *in* Christ from then. Now that is a great help because it means that everybody who has been baptised knows when it happened. You have got the date in your mind – that is when I was baptised, that is when I put off the old life, and that is when it was buried. That is when I took on the new life. That is my view of baptism: what God does in it is all-important, not what man is doing. That is why I make an appeal to everybody who has not been baptised as a believer to be baptised.

We had a 92-year-old lady who came to live in our home for the elderly in Chalfont St. Peter, Buckinghamshire, and you can see that lovely home to this day. We gave one room to this dear old lady. Frankly, the family simply wanted to be relieved of her. She was a great sport. She went running in her running shoes all around the big green in Chalfont St. Peter and had us all breathless watching her. Then one day she said to me: "Will you baptise me?"

I replied, "Why, what's brought this on?

She said, "I've realised that I'm a Christian and that this is a Christian place." She did not know when she came into our home for the elderly that it was a Christian place, but she knew it fairly quickly. Then she said: "I must be baptised; I must join the fellowship." I asked her which Sunday she would be free, and we put it in the diary that her baptism was going to be on that date. But it never was, because just two days before she was due to be baptised, she died and went to heaven. She was already in heaven and I am sure the Lord took it seriously that she wanted baptism, and she was so happy. So she went to the Lord with baptism firmly intended in her heart, and I am quite sure the Lord accepted that – not that she was a famous lady for having nursed with Florence Nightingale – and we sang hymns to her as she died. And She had an amazing past story, but she had not become a Christian earlier, even with all the goodness that was there. But then she became a Christian and immediately she asked for baptism and I am so glad that in her mind that was how to join – that was the way into the fellowship. She lived and died a baptised Christian.

Well now, that is radical because, in the average Christian circle, baptism is not counted that serious or that important and it has been a shock to some that I took it so seriously. But I do because Jesus gave us that and he ordered us to do it, and so to me it is not an optional extra, it is an absolute must. I think Paul is appealing to that as the moment when these things happened and claimed a new believer.

Read Colossians 3:18–4:18

I received a letter expressing thanks for the teaching on Colossians, saying "How hard it is to shake off the old man." I appreciated that very much because that is how we all ought to hear the word of God: doing something about it.

I am unhappy about starting this passage because the first part of it is: "Wives submit to your husbands as is fitting in the Lord." It is most surprising, and the whole block to the end of chapter 3 and into 4:1 is a kind of Pauline summary. You read that, word for word, in Ephesians as well, and you might ask why it is in two epistles. Why is it here? At first sight it does not seem fit. Your first reaction is to think that Paul got to the point of saying: there is not enough of me in this epistle; I will slip in what I wrote to the Ephesians. It might be that, but I think it is more. I think he is saying that relationships are the key to Christianity. Every relationship in life is needed here. And I think he knows something about the Colossians – that they need this. Anyway, for whatever reason it is there, and he says just the same thing wherever he preaches, and therefore for Paul this is vital.

There are three relationships in the home that every one of his readers has and he starts with those relationships. He starts with the underdog (if I dare say it) – with the one who has to submit. And he starts with the children and not the parents. He starts with the slaves and not their masters, which seems to be a funny thing to do. So he has got a word for everybody, but the critical word is first – for those who have the biggest job.

"Wives submit to your husbands as is fitting in the Lord"; and that word "Lord" now comes regularly – in every verse. Our very first study was about our Lord Jesus Christ and Paul has talked about Jesus Christ, but now it is *in* the Lord – as is fitting in the Lord. Children obey your parents in the Lord. All the way through, there is very practical counsel for people in their domestic relationships. You see, that is where we start in changing our relationships. They are the nearest and dearest to us, and if your faith does not start with the home, it is not starting properly. Therefore, if the home is all upside down, how dare you witness to your faith? Here is Paul's priority for the home. The first is a word to the wives and it is the most unpopular word today. We live in what is called an egalitarian society. That means an equal society when everybody wants to be equal with everybody else, and therefore this teaching of Paul to wives is anathema to our society when husbands and wives are in an equal democracy and have an equal vote on every issue. This is the Christian standard and though it is terribly unpopular, we have got to face up to it, that our home relationship began with the husband and wife and it began with the wife. The Greek word for "submit" means literally to put yourself under somebody.

Now, our society hates that. "We're all equal; nobody's under anybody else" – that is the mood which I encounter outside the church. Therefore it becomes doubly difficult to apply this, and yet it has to be applied.

In the traditional Book of Common Prayer wedding service of the Church of England, the bride's vows included a promise to obey her husband. (Twentieth century revised services made that word optional.) Husbands do not escape: "Husbands, love your wives." If you really love your wife, she will gladly submit to you. Mind you, she has to do that whether you love her or not. But it is a shame on you if you are not loving her in a way that makes it acceptable for her to submit. And: "Do not be harsh" with them. That is a funny word to put in there but it is a word for husbands. You are not to say: I've got a right that you submit to me. It is much better for the husband to say: I love you dearly; and then she says: I love you too, and I submit to you. It is a lovely thought, actually.

Let us move on to the next relationship: "Children, obey your parents in everything." You should ask them this, "For this pleases the Lord". Here is the key again. A household that is in the Lord will have all these relationships right. So you have to ask yourself: is my household of the Lord? Is it a household that he would walk into and say: Isn't this nice; isn't it lovely that I see a family like this? That is the key. If your children want to please the Lord they will obey you in everything, and it is the motivation that settles it.

Interestingly, Paul does not say "and you mothers don't embitter your children". He says, "you fathers", for the New Testament always looks to the father to settle relationships within a household, to discipline a household; and so mothers get off rather nicely at this point. But fathers set the tone for a family, and it is the fathers who are not to embitter their children. What a strange word to use; but I know from experience that you can, and that robs them of their motivation to obey you as father. Fathers, do not embitter your children or they will become discouraged – and that is the worst thing a father can do to his children, to discourage them.

Paul comes to the next relationship in the home: "Slaves, obey your earthly masters in everything." Now I don't have slaves in the household and nor do you. This is something we need to think through. To put it simply, does God abolish slavery? There was a lot of it in Arabia. When I was there,

I had meetings with slaves – a girl of nine was sold in the market for a hundred pounds and then taken into the bedroom as if she was a piece of furniture, and she was left in the bedroom until she died. That was pure slavery. She was probably an African, captured on the east coast of Africa, and brought up in a boat to Arabia, and there she was sold off. That was the first time I had any real contact with slavery. They used to love coming to the meetings we held because they were not part of the slavery situation and they had relief. It is no surprise to me that the biggest evangelism that is successful in the Middle East is among the slaves. They have responded to the gospel readily. So why didn't Paul say slavery is wrong and is against God's law? People have asked that, especially those who live in countries where there are slaves. Why does Paul apparently approve it? And we have got to have an answer.

Turn to 1 Timothy 1:10, "For adulterers and perverts, for slave traders and liars, perjurers". He is saying sinners include slave traders, so that you cannot accuse Paul of approving slavery when he puts that word into his letters. We can say that Paul puts slave traders among sinners. He classes them with adulterers and perverts. Thank you, Paul, for saying that. But why didn't Paul lead a rebellion of slaves against their masters? Why did he not try and kill slavery? Surely, that would be right.

We have got to be objective here. There were huge numbers of slaves in the Roman Empire. A slave was cheap; thirty pieces of silver would buy you a slave and from then on that slave was your property and you could do what you liked with a slave – they are your "thing". Paul would not have joined in slavery.

William Wilberforce began to agitate in Parliament for abolition. I wonder if you have seen the diagrams of ships that were in the slavery trade. They used to send the ships from Liverpool and Bristol all the way to West Africa and there were slaves there with which the ship was filled. That was when slavery was a trade and people were treated like objects and packed into slave ships. They had about 18 inches above their heads; they had to be pushed in like a slot and they were just packed in. They had no room at all and many of them died on the long journey to America, where they were sold so that the ship could fill up with sugar and come back to Bristol or Liverpool and traders would sell the sugar at a colossal profit. The cruelty on board those ships was terrible. They stank of themselves, they were just simply shoved in and then counted when they reached the West Indies to see how many had died during the voyage.

When you study slavery in the 18th Century, you then really discover why Christians – and it was Christians – rose up against it. The reason why it was such a battle in Britain was that many British people got the slave sugar and were in the trade and the profits were shared out. It was among people like us, and William Wilberforce said: I cannot stomach this as a Christian. The last letter that John Wesley ever wrote – and he was a great letter writer – was to Wilberforce to encourage him to fight on until he won in the House of Commons. That story is being made known now. It is coming out in films and in books, and some Christians are beginning to understand in a balanced way.

Actually, Paul was doing to the slave trade here something that would ultimately kill it: the relationship of masters and slaves was changed by Paul. So he was not accepting it – far from it. He was saying: both slave and master are "in the Lord". He is assuming it is a Christian household and that masters had done something about their own slaves. But he is concerned that slaves also do it right, so they are to obey their earthly masters, especially when the masters are not looking at them. Because slaves who are only working when the master looks at them are no good; they just don't do enough to earn their keep. So, whatever you do, work at it with all of your heart, throw yourself into your work. When the master wants something done, do it as if it was the Lord Jesus who had asked you to do it. The word "Lord" keeps coming in, and Paul is assuming that Christian owners of slaves have shared their religion with them and encouraged them to be "in the Lord".

Do you remember the letter to Philemon, the shortest letter Paul ever wrote? He was sending a slave back to his master, a slave who had run away into the anonymity of Rome and somehow met Paul and had become a Christian. You were pretty well bound to become a Christian if you worked for Paul. And that slave was "in the Lord", and so again it is a totally new relationship. That is acceptable to Paul. It is not something he would start a riot for. Christians through the ages would somehow inject their Christianity into the role of slaves. Christian householders probably had two slaves. They were cheap enough for them to do that. And so the majority of people in the Roman world were slaves. Many of them sold themselves to make a bit of money.

Anything people do that is wrong is recorded in heaven and there is a reward for that sort of thing and therefore that is injecting a very strong motivation into the relationship.

Ah, but just a minute. *Anyone* who does wrong will be punished, and that includes the master, and therefore he must remember that he has a Master in heaven and that Master is a very fair master who has no favouritism and of course, if you had a favourite slave, he would get a much better time.

Paul was actually killing slavery in the right way that would take centuries before it really worked. But it was Paul's letter to Philemon that called together a number of Christian clergy into a club for abolishing their slavery. That is the truth of it and that group of clergy was behind William

Wilberforce, encouraging him.

So: "Masters, provide your slaves with what is right and fair knowing that you also have a Master in heaven". We don't often think about Christ as our Master in heaven but that is what he is and therefore he has every right to tell us what to do. He is our Master. And Paul constantly refers to himself in his letters as "a bond slave of Jesus Christ". "Bond slave" is an extraordinary word for an apostle of Jesus Christ to use, but do you ever call yourself a bond slave? The word has even gone from our language. But that is what we are – we are all bond slaves. That means we are tied to him for life. What a word to use for a Christian. This passage is saying that when your home is "in the Lord" this is what it will be like.

The next section is on how we relate to outsiders. That word every Christian uses for people outside the church. How do we relate to outsiders? Paul is a master at relating to outsiders because he is chained to them, and I try to imagine what is it is like to be chained to Paul – who is literally chained to a soldier who must accompany him to everywhere he goes. You are chained, and your chains make a noise, rattling. That is what Paul was – a prisoner in a house, chained to a Roman soldier. That soldier was on duty every minute of the day. Therefore, Paul knew how to approach outsiders, chained to one of them. That is why the gospel got right into Caesar's household – because people prayed when someone was in prison for Christ. But they usually prayed for the wrong thing.

There were a number of Indians who were imprisoned for the gospel and the church in India heard about them and said, "We must pray for them." A group of Indian Christians got together and prayed for those in prison in Nepal. Now what did they pray for? They prayed for their comfort, they prayed for their release – all good Christian prayers – until it came round to a little old lady who said, "Lord, why did you give them the privilege of being imprisoned for you?" Suddenly, the whole atmosphere of the prayer room changed. They realised what they should have been praying for. Paul is saying here, in 4:2–4 that God would open a door for the word, "to declare the mystery of Christ", on account of which he was in prison. What a wonderful opportunity – to be chained to an outsider. He had learned how to relate to them. Sure enough, many of those soldiers became Christians and in the household of the Roman emperor himself there were outsiders who were led to the Lord by Paul.

What do you do to talk to an outsider? You pray that you may share the gospel and share it clearly and lovingly; all that is here. Paul doesn't moan about being chained to someone. To him it is an exciting opportunity. They can't get away from you. That is just what a Christian wants, and frequently he led to the Lord soldiers with whom he was chained. So: pray that I may open a door for my message and pray that I may tell it clearly as I should, proclaim the mystery of Christ for which I am in chains.

Now there is a simple prayer for you when a Christian is in real trouble. They will be in trouble from outsiders and that gives them an opportunity. He says: be wise in the way you act towards outsiders; make the most of every opportunity.

As a young man, I went to a big crusade in Wales and there was an older man called Tom assigned to work with me in a big crusade. He was a wonderful man. He was in his sixties, and I think he was retired, but we would walk down a street in Wales and there would be an outsider and Tom knew exactly how to speak to that person. He was always so right that he was immediately in touch with their spirits. I wasn't; I just was there, watching and learning. But what a gracious man he was – a very ordinary man, but he had the gift of talking to outsiders. It must be a real gift because it is not all that common. I am afraid when we spend so much time with "insiders", we lose the gift of talking to outsiders. People lose it about three years after they come to Christ, and from then on they know exactly how to talk to brethren, and they have lost the ability to communicate with people they worked with. Let us pray that God will keep that gift in us, and we shall not lose it. That is opening doors for the message.

So he says: let your conversation be always "full of grace" – I think I understand that – and "seasoned with salt." I don't understand that. I get that it is important "so that you may know how to answer everyone." That gift is part of this gift of communication.

Finally, there is another set of relationships which Christians need and that is why epistles in the New Testament finish with greetings. That is not a coincidence; it is not just a nice way to end a letter. It is saying to Christians: you have an important duty to relate to your fellow Christians, to as many as possible. That, again, is part of putting relationships right.

I hope you have relationships with your fellow Christians at some level and be able to pass on greetings as you may. Let us look at some of the greetings Paul passes on. "Tychicus will tell you all the news about me". He was sending him deliberately to give them news about him which would enable them to relate to him more deeply. He is "a dear brother, faithful minister, fellow servant in the Lord; I am sending him to visit for the express purpose that you may know everything concerning me and be encouraged in your hearts." Paul also says, "I am sending him along to you with Onesimus". There is the man himself, the slave who Paul sent back to his master. His name, Onesimus, meant "useful" and Paul picks that up in his letter. He is saying: you may not have found him useful in the past but you will find him useful in the present, and he is now a brother in the Lord.

That would make a whole difference.

"My fellow prisoner Aristarchus sends you his greetings and so does Mark a cousin of Barnabas." Behind that one word "Mark" is a difficulty Paul himself had because Mark he took on a missionary journey and I am afraid he did not make it. He was just not up to Paul and it was one of the difficulties Paul had in his early ministry that he had Mark tag along and he finally got rid of him, sent him packing. Amazing. But now he is sending Mark greetings and he hints: you probably heard about his life; I am telling you, don't pay any attention to what you hear; you must welcome him. He is a good brother now and I can vouch for him. He says: you have received instruction about him, but if he comes to you, welcome him. Because if people knew that Paul had rejected him, they rejected Mark. He is now a brother, and if he comes to you, welcome him.

Then, a funny thing, he says Jesus is coming. But this is not the Jesus you have heard about. Do you know there are a number of Jesuses in the New Testament? But he says: Jesus who is called Justus. That means they had another name for him. It was a nickname of some kind, but it is a nice nickname to have. Jesus who is called Justus also sends greetings. Now that is a unique thing. Paul, writing in one of his letters, commends Jesus to them, but not the one you are thinking of. Jesus the Just, and that fits him. Then he says, now these are the only Jews who are with me. There were three Jews who visited Paul in Rome and those were the three. It really encouraged him.

Who is the next? "Epaphras who is one of you...." We know from chapter 1 that Epaphras started the church and won them all for Christ and then let them be a church. So Epaphras is greeting them and "he is always wrestling for you in prayer" – that you may stand and fully assured, mature. I vouch for him that he is still working hard for you in our little prayer group that we have, and he is always praying for you, his children. That was one of the reasons they kept up. Then, he said, he is working for those at Laodicea and Hierapolis. Those are two places very near to where they were. Paul is working for them even though he has never seen them, never been there. Then he refers to Luke, the doctor. I think it is lovely that God arranged a doctor to accompany Paul on most of his journeys. When he was whipped within an inch of his life, there was a doctor there to care for the wounds. I am sorry to tell you that the next name was a disappointment – Demas. Demas is mentioned in another letter as being not worthy of his Christian calling. Still, Demas was here sending greetings, but I am afraid a little later he fell. It is interesting that Paul is so honest about people. He praises them and he does the opposite when they have let him down.

Laodicea and Hierapolis, both of which I have been to, were churches founded by Phillip, one of the twelve. Then here is a little word of correction. "Tell Archippus ... see to it that you complete the work you have received in the Lord." I would not like to be that man with that read out in a letter from Paul. It implied very seriously: you are not doing the job the Lord gave you. That would be a particularly unpleasant thing to know – that all the people who are hearing the letter read would hear about Archippus.

Then: "I, Paul, write this greeting in my own hand". I am quite sure there would be people who would like Paul's signature, but he is not pleasing autograph hunters. Why does he sign it in his own hand? Well, it is more personal than if he didn't; he has probably dictated the whole letter to a secretary or an "amanuensis" as they called them, but it was also a safeguard. Already by that time, other people were writing letters in his name and when it had his signature in very large, straggly letters it protected that letter from people who would imitate him. The message is: you need to finish the work God gave you, and I send you this greeting in my own hand. That tells us possibly that his great handicap in the flesh was blindness, and its start would have been as the result of that meeting with the Lord on the road to Damascus which literally blinded him, and it could have so damaged his eyes that there was something wrong with them. That is my theory but he certainly had something wrong with his eyes because he wrote in the most extraordinary spirit; and then he said: "Remember my chains." That is the 3rd time he has mentioned them in this letter. If you were chained to a Roman soldier, you would think of them. I would not like to be chained with Paul. He would very quickly sort me out. But the soldiers were sorted out.

Then there is his final "Grace be with you." That word "grace" I have been speaking about quite a bit lately because it has got three different meanings among Christians today, two of which are wrong. The three meanings of grace have become these: *unconditional forgiveness*; *undeserved favour* (which is the real meaning), and *irresistible force*. That is a terrible abuse of the word "grace" because it is a very beautiful word.

In scripture it means *undeserved favour*. Paul is the only one who really uses the word "grace" and he was such an example of grace that he could not get over it – that he, who began life as an anti-Christian missionary, set out to put them all in prison, met Jesus of Nazareth on the way. The result is what we know. I had to speak on grace in Singapore because there were some examples of pastors preaching the wrong kind of grace and filling their churches. It almost hurt me that the word grace was being so misused, but the pastor who was misusing it as unconditional forgiveness was teaching that when you came to Christ all your sins were forgiven including all the ones that you were *going to* sin. That was just one aspect of it that was terribly wrong. It virtually gave you a free pass into the world of sin and it was not the gospel.

Another misuse was *irresistible force*. Misusing texts like "By grace are you saved" it seemed as if God had a grace that was irresistible – you could do nothing about it. Yet all the records of the New Testament show that you can resist grace. It is not an irresistible force.

When Paul says "Grace be with you" he is thinking of himself, because if ever anybody knew the grace of God, it was Paul – that he, formerly the hater of Christians, should be the most amazing missionary that God has ever had. It is sheer grace.

The great letter of Paul to the Colossians is not everyone's favourite, it is not one that you normally think of as your favourite, but it has become mine.

www.ingramcontent.com/pod-product-compliance
Lightning Source LLC
Chambersburg PA
CBHW071531080526
44588CB00011B/1634